Of Crimes and Punishments

Cesare Beccaria-Bonesana

Copyright Notice

TABLE OF CONTENTS

Introduction

In every human society, there is an effort continually tending to confer on one part the height of power and happiness, and to reduce the other to the extreme of weakness and misery. The intent of good laws is to oppose this effort, and to diffuse their influence universally and equally. But men generally abandoned the care of their most important concerns to the uncertain prudence and discretion of those whose interest it is to reject the best and wisest institutions; and it is not till they have been led into a thousand mistakes in matters the most essential to their lives and liberties, and are weary of suffering, that they can be induced to apply a remedy to the evils with which they are oppressed. It is then they begin to conceive and acknowledge the most palpable truths which, from their very simplicity, commonly escape vulgar minds, incapable of analysing objects, accustomed to receive impressions, without distinction, and to be determined rather by the opinions of others than by the result of their own examination.

II

If we look into history we shall find that laws, which are, or ought to be, conventions between men in a state of freedom. have been, for the most part the work of the passions of a few, or the consequences of a fortuitous or temporary necessity; not dictated by a cool examiner of human nature, who knew how to collect in one point the actions of a multitude, and had this only end in view, the greatest happiness of the greatest number. Happy are those few nations who have not waited till the slow succession of human vicissitudes should, from the extremity of evil, produce a transition to good; but by prudent laws have facilitated the progress from one to the other! And how great are the obligations due from mankind to that philosopher, who, from the obscurity of his closet, had the courage to scatter among the multitude the seeds of useful truths, so long unfruitful!

The art of printing has diffused the knowledge of those philosophical truths, by which the relations between sovereigns and their subjects, and between nations are discovered. By this knowledge commerce is animated, and there has sprung up a spirit of emulation and industry, worthy of rational beings. These are the produce of this enlightened age; but the cruelty of punishments, and the irregularity of proceedings in criminal cases, so principal a part of the legislation, and so much neglected throughout Europe, has hardly ever been called in question. Efforts, accumulated through many centuries, have never yet been exposed by ascending to general principles; nor has the force of acknowledged truths been ever opposed to the unbounded licentiousness of ill-directed power, which has continually produced so many authorised examples of the most unfeeling barbarity. Surely, the groans of the weak, sacrificed to the cruel ignorance and indolence of the powerful, the barbarous torments lavished, and multiplied with useless severity, for crimes either not proved, or in their nature impossible, the filth and horrors of a prison, increased by the most cruel tormentor of the miserable, uncertainty, ought to have roused the attention of those whose business is to direct the opinions of mankind.

The immortal Montesquieu has but slightly touched on this subject. Truth, which is eternally the same, has obliged me to follow the steps of that great man; but the studious part of mankind, for whom I write, will easily distinguish the superstructure from the foundation. I shall be happy if, with him,

IV

I can obtain the secret thanks of the obscure and peaceful disciples of reason and philosophy, and excite that tender emotion in which sensible minds sympathise with him who pleads the cause of humanity.

Of the Origin of Punishments

***

Laws are the conditions under which men, naturally independent, united themselves in society. Weary of living in a continual state of war, and of enjoying a liberty which became of little value, from the uncertainty of its duration, they sacrificed one part of it, to enjoy the rest in peace and security. The sum of all these portions of the liberty of each individual constituted the sovereignty of a nation and was deposited in the hands of the sovereign, as the lawful administrator. But it was not sufficient only to establish this deposit; it was also necessary to defend it from the usurpation of each individual, who will always endeavour to take away from the mass, not only his own portion, but to encroach on that of others. Some motives therefore, that strike the senses were necessary to prevent the despotism of each individual from plunging society into its former chaos. Such motives are the punishments established, against the infractors of the laws. I say that motives of this kind are necessary; because experience shows, that the multitude adopt no established principle of conduct; and because society is prevented from approaching to that dissolution, (to which, as well

as all other parts of the physical and moral world, it naturally tends,) only by motives that are the immediate objects of sense, and which being continually presented to the mind, are sufficient to counterbalance the effects of the passions of the individual which oppose the general good. Neither the power of eloquence nor the sublimest truths are sufficient to restrain, for any length of time, those passions which are excited by the lively impressions of present objects.

Of the right to punish

***

Every punishment which does not arise from absolute necessity, says the great Montesquieu, is tyrannical. A proposition which may be made more general thus: every act of authority of one man over another, for which there is not an absolute necessity, is tyrannical. It is upon this then that the sovereign's right to punish crimes is founded; that is, upon the necessity of defending the public liberty, entrusted to his care, from the usurpation of individuals; and punishments are just in proportion, as the liberty, preserved by the sovereign, is sacred and valuable.

Let us consult the human heart, and there we shall find the foundation of the sovereign's right to punish; for no advantage in moral policy can be lasting which is not founded on the indelible sentiments of the heart of man. Whatever law deviates from this principle will always meet with a resistance which will destroy it in the end; for the smallest force continually applied will overcome the most violent motion communicated to bodies.

No man ever gave up his liberty merely for the good of the public. Such a chimera exists only in romances. Every individual wishes, if possible, to be exempt from the compacts that bind the rest of mankind.

The multiplication of mankind, though slow, being too great, for the means which the earth, in its natural state, offered to satisfy necessities which every day became more numerous, obliged men to separate again, and form new societies. These naturally opposed the first, and a state of war was transferred from individuals to nations.

Thus it was necessity that forced men to give up apart of their liberty. It is certain, then, that every individual would choose to put into the public stock the smallest portion possible, as much only as was sufficient to engage others to defend it. The aggregate of these, the smallest portions possible, forms the right of punishing; all that extends beyond this, is abuse, not justice.

Observe that by justice I understand nothing more than that bond which is necessary to keep the interest of individuals united, without which men would return to their original state of barbarity.

All punishments which exceed the necessity of preserving this bond are in their nature unjust. We should be cautious how we associate with the word justice an idea of any thing real, such as a physical power, or a being that actually exists. I do not, by any means, speak of the justice of God, which is of another kind, and refers immediately to rewards and punishments in a life to come.

Consequences of the foregoing Principles

***

The laws only can determine the punishment of crimes; and the authority of making penal laws can only reside with the legislator, who represents the whole society united by the social compact. No magistrate then, (as he is one of the society,) can, with justice, inflict on any other member of the same society punishment that is not ordained by the laws. But as a punishment, increased beyond the degree fixed by the law, is the just punishment with the addition of another, it follows that no magistrate, even under a pretence of zeal, or the public good, should increase the punishment already determined by the laws.

If every individual be bound to society, society is equally bound to him, by a contract which from its nature equally binds both parties. This obligation, which descends from the throne to the cottage, and equally binds the highest and lowest of mankind, signifies nothing more than that it is the interest of all, that conventions, which are useful to the greatest number, should be punctually observed. The violation of this compact by any individual is an introduction to anarchy.

The sovereign, who represents the society itself, can only make general laws to bind the members; but it belongs not to him to judge whether any individual has violated the social compact, or incurred the punishment in consequence. For in this case there are two parties, one represented by the sovereign, who insists upon the violation of the contract, and the other is the person accused who denies it. It is necessary then that there should be a third person to decide this contest; that is to say, a judge, or magistrate, from whose determination there should be no appeal; and this determination should consist of a simple affirmation or negation of fact.

If it can only be proved, that the severity of punishments, though not immediately contrary to the public good, or to the end for which they were intended, viz. to prevent crimes, be useless, then such severity would be contrary to those beneficent virtues, which are the consequence of enlightened reason, which instructs the sovereign to wish rather to govern men in a state of freedom and happiness than of slavery. It would also be contrary to justice and the social compact.

Of the Interpretation of Laws

***

Judges, in criminal cases, have no right to interpret the penal laws, because they are not legislators. They have not received the laws from our ancestors as a domestic tradition, or as the will of a testator, which his heirs and executors are to obey; but they receive them from a society actually existing, or from the sovereign, its representative. Even the authority of the laws is not founded on any pretended obligation, or ancient convention; which must be null, as it cannot bind those who did not exist at the time of its institution; and unjust, as it would reduce men in the ages following, to a herd of brutes, without any power of judging or acting. The laws receive their force and authority from an oath of fidelity, either tacit or expressed, which living subjects have sworn to their sovereign, in order to restrain the intestine fermentation of the private interest of individuals. From hence springs their true and natural authority. Who then is their lawful interpreter? The sovereign, that is, the representative of society, and not the judge, whose office is only to examine if a man have or have not committed an action contrary to the laws.

In every criminal cause the judge should reason syllogistically. The major should be the general law; the minor, the conformity of the action, or its opposition to the laws; the conclusion, liberty, or punishment. If the judge be obliged by the imperfection of the laws, or chooses to make any other or more syllogisms than this, it will be an introduction to uncertainty.

There is nothing more dangerous than the common axiom, the spirit of the laws is to be considered. To adopt it is to give way to the torrent of opinions. This may seem a paradox to vulgar minds, which are more strongly affected by the smallest disorder before their eyes, than by the most pernicious though remote consequences produced by one false principle adopted by a nation.

Our knowledge is in proportion to the number of our ideas. The more complex these are, the greater is the variety of positions in which they may be considered. Every man hath his own particular point of view, and, at different times, sees the same objects in very different lights. The spirit of the laws will then be the result of the good or bad logic of the judge; and this will depend on his good or bad digestion, on the violence of his passions, on the rank or condition. of the accused, or on his connections with the judge, and on all those little circumstances which change the appearance of objects in the fluctuating mind of man. Hence we see the fate of a delinquent changed many times in passing through the different courts of judicature, and his life and liberty victims to the false ideas or ill humour of the judge, who mistakes the vague result of his own confused reasoning for the just interpretation of the laws. We see the same crimes punished in a different manner at different times in the same tribunals, the consequence of not having consulted the constant and invariable voice of the laws, but the erring instability of arbitrary interpretation.

The disorders that may arise from a rigorous observance of the letter of penal laws are not to be compared with those produced by the interpretation of them. The first are temporary inconveniences which will oblige the legislature to correct the letter of the law, the want of preciseness and uncertainty of which has occasioned these disorders; and this will put a stop to the fatal liberty of explaining, the source of arbitrary and venal declamations. When the code of laws is once fixed, it should be observed in the literal sense, and nothing more is left to the judge than to determine whether an action be or be not conformable to the written law. When the rule of right, which ought to direct the actions of the philosopher, as well as the ignorant, is a matter of controversy, not of fact, the people are slaves to the magistrates. The despotism of this multitude of tyrants is more insupportable the less the distance is between the oppressor and the oppressed, more fatal than that of one, for the tyranny of many is not to be shaken off but by having recourse to that of one alone. It is more cruel, as it meets with more opposition, and the cruelty of a tyrant is not in proportion to his strength, but to the obstacles that oppose him.

These are the means by which security of person and property is best obtained, which is just, as it is the purpose of uniting in society; and it is useful as each person may calculate exactly the inconveniences attending every crime. By these means, subjects will acquire a spirit of independence and liberty, however it may appear to those who dare to call the weakness of submitting blindly to their capricious and interested opinions by the sacred name of virtue.

These principles will displease those who have made it a rule with themselves to transmit to their inferiors the tyranny they suffer from their superiors. I should have every thing to fear if tyrants were to read my book; but tyrants never read.

Of the Obscurity of Laws

***

If the power of interpreting laws be an evil, obscurity in them must be another, as the former is the consequence of the latter. This evil will be still greater if the laws be written in a language unknown to the people; who, being ignorant of the consequences of their own actions, become necessarily dependent on a few, who are interpreters of the laws, which, instead of being public and general, are thus rendered private and particular. What must we think of mankind when we reflect, that such is the established custom of the greatest part of our polished and enlightened Europe? Crimes will be less frequent in proportion as the code of laws is more universally read and understood; for there is no doubt but that the eloquence of the passions is greatly assisted by the ignorance and uncertainty of punishments.

Hence it follows, that, without written laws, no society will ever acquire a fixed form of government, in which the power is vested in the whole, and not in any part of the society; and in which the laws are not to be altered but by the will of the whole, nor corrupted by the force of private interest. Experience and reason show us that the probability of human traditions diminishes in proportion as they are distant from. their sources. How then can laws resist the inevitable force of time, if there be not a lasting monument of the social compact.

Hence we see the use of printing, which alone makes the public, and not a few individuals, the guardians and defenders of the laws. It is this art which by diffusing literature, has gradually dissipated the gloomy spirit of cabal and intrigue. To this art it is owing that the atrocious crimes of our ancestors, who were alternately slaves and tyrants, are become less frequent. Those who are acquainted with the history of the two or three last centuries may observe, how from the lap of luxury and effeminacy have sprung the most tender virtues, humanity, benevolence, and toleration of human errors. They may contemplate the effects of what was so improperly called ancient simplicity and good faith; humanity groaning under implacable superstition, the avarice and ambition of a few staining with human blood the drones and palaces of kings, secret treasons and public massacres, every noble a tyrant over the people, and the ministers of the gospel of Christ bathing their

hands in blood in the name of the God of all mercy. We may talk as we please of the corruption and degeneracy of the present age, but happily we see no such horrid examples of cruelty and oppression.

Of the Proportion between Crimes and Punishments

***

It is not only the common interest of mankind that crimes should not be committed, but that crimes of every kind should be less frequent, in proportion to the evil they produce to society. Therefore the means made use of by the legislature to prevent crimes should be more powerful in proportion as they are destructive of the public safety and happiness, and as the inducements to commit them are stronger. Therefore there ought to be a fixed proportion between crimes and punishments.

It is impossible to prevent entirely all the disorders which the passions of mankind cause in society. These disorders increase in proportion to the number of people and the opposition of private interests. If we consult history, we shall find them increasing, in every state, with the extent of dominion. In political arithmetic, it is necessary to substitute a calculation of probabilities to mathematical exactness. That force which continually impels us to our own private interest, like gravity, acts incessantly, unless it meets with an obstacle to oppose it. The effect of this force are the confused series of human actions. Punishments, which

I would call political obstacles, prevent the fatal effects of private interest, without destroying the impelling cause, which is that sensibility inseparable from man. The legislator acts, in this case, like a skilful architect, who endeavours to counteract the force of gravity by combining the circumstances which may contribute to the strength of his edifice.

The necessity of uniting in society being granted, together with the conventions which the opposite interests of individuals must necessarily require, a scale of crimes may be formed, of which the first degree should consist of those which immediately tend to the dissolution of society, and the last of the smallest possible injustice done to a private member of that society. Between these extremes will be comprehended all actions contrary to the public good which are called criminal, and which descend by insensible degrees, decreasing from the highest to the lowest. If mathematical calculation could be applied to the obscure and infinite combinations of human actions, there might be a corresponding scale of punishments, descending from the greatest to the least; but it will be sufficient that the wise legislator mark the principal divisions, without disturbing the order, left to crimes of the first degree be assigned punishments of the last. If there were an exact and universal scale of crimes and punishments, we should there have a common measure of the degree of liberty and slavery, humanity and cruelty of different nations.

Any action which is not comprehended in the above mentioned scale will not be called a crime, or punished as such, except by those who have an interest in the denomination. The uncertainty of the extreme points of this scale hath produced system of morality which contradicts the laws, multitude of laws that contradict each other, and many which expose the best men to the severest punishments, rendering the ideas of vice and virtue vague and fluctuating and even their existence doubtful. Hence that fatal lethargy of political bodies, which terminates in their destruction.

Whoever reads, with a philosophic eye, the history of nations, and their laws, will generally find, that the ideas of virtue and vice, of a good or bad citizen, change with the revolution of ages, not in proportion to the alteration of circumstances, and consequently conformable to the common good, but in proportion to the passions and errors by which the different lawgivers were successively influenced. He will frequently observe that the passions and vices of one age are the foundation of the morality of the following; that violent passion, the offspring of fanaticism and enthusiasm, being weakened by time, which reduces all the phenomena of the natural and moral world to an equality, become, by degrees, the prudence of the age, and an useful instrument in the hands of the powerful or artful politician. Hence the uncertainty of our notions of honour and virtue; an uncertainty which will ever remain, because they change with the revolutions of time, and names survive the things they originally signified; they change with the boundaries of states, which are often the same both in physical and moral geography.

Pleasure and pain are the only springs of actions in beings endowed with sensibility. Even amongst the motives which incite men to acts of religion, the invisible legislator has ordained rewards and punishments. From a partial distribution of these will arise that contradiction, so little observed, because so common, I mean that of punishing by the laws the crimes which the laws have occasioned. If an equal punishment be ordained for

two crimes that injure society in different degrees, there is nothing to deter men from committing the greater as often as it is attended with greater advantage.

Of estimating the Degree of Crimes

***

The foregoing reflections authorise me to assert that crimes are only to be measured by the injury done to society.

They err, therefore, who imagine that a crime is greater or less according to the intention of the person by whom it is committed; for this will depend on the actual impression of objects on the senses, and on the previous disposition of the mind; both which will vary in different persons, and even in the same person at different times according to the succession of ideas, passions, and circumstances. Upon that system it would be necessary to form, not only a particular code for every individual, but a new penal law for every crime. Men, often with the best intention, do the greatest injury to society, and, with the worst, do it the most essential services.

Others have estimated crimes rather by the dignity of the person offended than by their consequences to society. If this were the true standard, the smallest irreverence to the Divine Being ought to be punished with infinitely more severity than the assassination of a monarch.

In short, others have imagined, that the greatness of the sin should aggravate the crime. But the fallacy of this opinion will appear on the slightest consideration of the relations between man and man, and between God and man. The relations between man and man are relations of equality. Necessity alone hath produced, from the opposition of private passions and interests, the idea of public utility, which is the foundation of human justice. The other are relations of dependence, between an imperfect creature and his Creator, the most perfect of beings, who has reserved to himself the sole right of being both lawgiver and judge; for he alone can, without injustice, be, at the same time, both one and the other. If he hath decreed eternal punishments for those who disobey his will, shall an insect dare to put himself in the place of divine justice, or pretend to punish for the Almighty, who is himself all sufficient, who cannot receive impressions of pleasure or pain, and who alone, of all other beings, acts without being acted upon? The degree of sin depends on the malignity of the heart, which is impenetrable to finite beings. How then can the degree of sin serve as a standard to determine the degree of crimes? If that were admitted, men may punish when God pardons, and pardon when God condemns; and thus act in opposition to the Supreme Being.

Of the Division of Crimes

***

We have proved then, that crimes are to be estimated by the injury done to society. This is one of those palpable truths which though evident to the meanest capacity, yet by a combination of circumstances, are only known to a few thinking men in every nation, and in every age. But opinions, worthy only of the despotism of Asia, and passions, armed with power and authority, have, generally by insensible, and sometimes by violent impressions on the timid credulity of men, effaced those simple ideas which perhaps constituted the first philosophy of an infant society. Happily the philosophy of the present enlightened age seems again to conduct us to the same principles, and with that degree of certainty which is obtained by a rational examination and repeated experience.

A scrupulous adherence to order would require, that we should now examine and distinguish the different species of crimes and the modes of punishment; but they are so variable in their nature, from the different circumstances of ages and countries, that the detail would be tiresome and endless. It will be sufficient for my purpose to point out the most general principles, and the most common and dangerous errors, in order to undeceive as well those who, from a mistaken zeal for liberty, would introduce anarchy and confusion, as those who pretend to reduce society in general to the regularity of a covenant.

Some crimes are immediately destructive of society, or its representative; others attack the private security of the life, property, or honour of individuals; and a third class consists of such actions as are contrary to the laws which relate to the general good of the community.

The first, which are of the highest degree, as they are most destructive to society, are called crimes of leze-majesty (High Treason). Tyranny and ignorance, which have confounded the clearest terms and ideas, have given this appellation to crimes of a different nature, and consequently have established the same punishment for each; and, on this occasion, as on a thousand others, men have been sacrificed victims to a word. Every crime, even of the most private nature, injures society; but every crime does not threaten its immediate destruction. Moral as well as physical actions have their sphere of activity differently circumscribed, like all the movements of nature, by time and space; it is therefore a sophistical interpretation, the common philosophy of slaves, that would confound the limits of things established by eternal truth.

To these succeed crimes which are destructive of the security of individuals. This security being the principal end of all society, and to which every citizen hath an undoubted right, it becomes indispensably necessary, that to these crimes the greatest of punishments should be assigned.

The opinion, that every member of society has a right to do any thing that is not contrary to the laws, without fearing any other inconveniences than those which are the natural consequences of the action itself, is a political dogma, which should be defended by the laws, inculcated by the magistrates, and believed by the people; a sacred dogma, without which there can be no lawful society, a just recompense for our sacrifice of that universal liberty of action common to all sensible beings, and only limited by our natural powers. By this principle our minds become free, active, and vigorous; by this alone we are inspired with that virtue which knows no fear, so different from that pliant prudence, worthy of those only who can bear a precarious existence.

Attempts, therefore, against the life and liberty of a citizen are crimes of the highest nature. Under this head we comprehend not only assassinations and robberies committed by the populace, but by grandees and magistrates, whose example acts with more force, and at a greater distance destroying the ideas of justice and duty among the subjects, and substituting that of the right of the strongest, equally dangerous to those who exercise it and to those who suffer.

Of Honour

***

There is a remarkable difference between the civil laws, those jealous guardians of life and property, and the laws of what is called honour, which particularly respects the opinion of others. Honour is a term which has been the foundation of many long and brilliant reasonings, without annexing to it any precise or fixed idea. How miserable is the condition of the human mind, to which the most distant and least essential matters, the revolutions of the heavenly bodies, are more distinctly known than the most interesting truths of morality, which are always confused and fluctuating, as they happen to be driven by the gales of passion, or received and transmitted by ignorance! But this will cease to appear strange, if it be considered, that as objects, when too near the eye appear confused, so the too great vicinity of the ideas of morality is the reason why the simple ideas of which they are composed are easily confounded, but which must be separated before we can investigate the phenomena of human sensibility; and the intelligent observer of human nature will cease to be surprised, that so many ties, and such an apparatus of morality, are necessary to the security and happiness of mankind.

Honour, then, is one of those complex ideas which are an aggregate not only of simple ones, but of others so complicated, that, in their various modes of affecting the human mind, they sometimes admit and sometimes exclude part of the elements of which they are composed, retaining only some few of the most common, as many algebraic quantities admit one common divisor. To find this common divisor of the different ideas attached to the word honour, it will be necessary to go back to the original formation of society.

The first laws and the first magistrates owed their existence to the necessity of preventing the disorders which the natural despotism of individuals would unavoidably produce. This was the object of the establishment of society, and was, either in reality or in appearance, the principal design of all codes of laws, even the most pernicious. But the more intimate connexions of men, and the progress of their knowledge, gave rise to an infinite number of necessities and mutual acts of friendship between the members of society. These necessities were not foreseen by the laws, and could not be satisfied by the actual power of each individual. At this epoch began to be established the despotism of opinion, as being the only means of obtaining those benefits which the law could not procure, and of removing those evils against which the laws were no security. It is opinion, that tormentor of the wise and the ignorant, that has exalted the appearance of virtue above virtue itself. Hence the esteem of men becomes not only useful but necessary to every one, to prevent his sinking below the common level. The ambitious man grasps at it, as being necessary to his designs; the vain man sues for it, as a testimony of his merit; the honest man demands it, as his due; and most men consider it as necessary to their existence.

Honour, being produced after the formation of society, could not be a part of the common deposite, and therefore, whilst we act under its influence, we return, for that instant, to a state of nature and withdraw ourselves from the laws, which, in this case, are insufficient for our protection.

Hence it follows, that, in extreme political liberty, and in absolute despotism, all ideas of honour disappear, or are confounded with others. In the first case, reputation becomes useless from the despotism of the laws; and in the second, the despotism of one man, annulling all civil existence, reduces the rest to a precarious and temporary personality. Honour, then, is one of the fundamental principles of those monarchies which are a limited despotism; and in those, like revolutions in despotic states, it is a momentary return to state of nature and original equality.

Of Duelling

***

From the necessity of the esteem of others have arisen single combats, and they have been established by the anarchy of the laws. They are thought to have been unknown to the ancients, perhaps because they did not assemble in their temples, in their theatres, or with their friends, suspiciously armed with swords; and, perhaps, because single combats were a common spectacle, exhibited to the people by gladiators, who were slaves, and whom freemen disdained to imitate.

In vain have the laws endeavoured to abolish this custom by punishing the offenders with death. A man of honour, deprived of the esteem of others, foresees that be must be reduced either to a solitary existence, insupportable to a social creature, or become the object of perpetual insult; considerations sufficient to overcome the fear of death.

What is the reason that duels are not so frequent among the common people as amongst the great? not only because they do not wear swords, but because to men of that class reputation is of less importance than it is to those of a higher rank, who commonly regard each other with distrust and jealousy.

It may not be without its use to repeat here what has been mentioned by other writers, viz. that the best method of preventing this crime is to punish the aggressor, that is, the person who gave occasion to the duel, and to acquit him who, without any fault on his side, is obliged to defend that which is not sufficiently secured to him by the laws.

Of crimes which disturb the Public Tranquillity

***

Another class of crimes are those which disturb the public tranquillity and the quiet of the citizens; such as tumults and riots in the public streets, which are intended for commerce and the passage of the inhabitants; the discourses of fanatics, which rouse the passions of the curious multitude, and gain strength from the number of their hearers, who, though deaf to calm and solid reasoning, are always affected by obscure and mysterious enthusiasm.

The illumination of the streets during the night at the public expense, guards stationed in different quarters of the city, the plain and moral discourses of religion reserved for the silence and tranquillity of churches, and protected by authority, and harangues in support of the interest of the public, delivered only at the general meetings of the nation, in parliament, or where the sovereign resides, are all means to prevent the dangerous effects of the misguided passions of the people. These should be the principal objects of the vigilance of a magistrate, and which the French call police; but if this magistrate should act in an arbitrary manner, and not in conformity to the code of laws) which ought to be in the hands of every member of the community, he opens a door to tyranny, which always surrounds the confines of political liberty.

I do not know of any exception to this general axiom, that Every member of society should know when he is criminal and when innocent. If censors, and, in general, arbitrary magistrates, be necessary in any government, it proceeds from some fault in the constitution. The uncertainty of crimes hath sacrificed more victims to secret tyranny than have ever suffered by public and solemn cruelty.

What are, in general, the proper punishments for crimes? Is the punishment of death really useful, or necessary for the safety or good order of society? Are tortures and torments consistent with justice, or do they answer the end proposed by the laws? Which is the best method of preventing crimes? Are the same punishments equally useful at all times? What influence have they on manners? These problems should be solved with that geometrical precision, which the mist of sophistry, the seduction of eloquence, and the timidity of doubt, are unable to resist. if I have no other merit than that of having first presented to my country, with a greater degree of evidence, what other nations have written and are beginning to practice, I shall account myself fortunate; but if by supporting the rights of mankind and of invincible truth, I shall contribute to save from the agonies of death one unfortunate victim of tyranny, or of ignorance, equally fatal, his blessing and tears of transport will be a sufficient consolation to me for the contempt of all mankind.

Of the Intent of Punishments

***

From the foregoing considerations it is evident that the intent of punishments is not to torment a sensible being, nor to undo a crime already committed. Is it possible that torments and useless cruelty, the instrument of furious fanaticism or the impotency of tyrants, can be authorised by a political body, which, so far from being influenced by passion, should be the cool moderator of the passions of individuals? Can the groans of a tortured wretch recall the time past, or reverse the crime he has committed?

The end of punishment, therefore, is no other than to prevent the criminal from doing further injury to society, and to prevent others from committing the like offence. Such punishments, therefore, and such a mode of inflicting them, ought to be chosen, as will make the strongest and most lasting impressions on the minds of others, with the least torment to the body of the criminal.

Of the Credibility of Witnesses

***

To determine exactly the credibility of a witness, and the force of evidence, is an important point in every good legislation. Every man of common sense, that is, every one whose ideas have some connection with each other, and whose sensations are conformable to those of other men, may be a witness; but the credibility of his evidence will be in proportion as he is interested in declaring or concealing the truth. Hence it appears how frivolous is the reasoning of those who reject the testimony of women, on account of their weakness; how puerile it is not to admit the evidence of those who are under sentence of death, because they are dead in law; and how irrational to exclude persons branded with infamy; for in all these cases they ought to be credited, when they have no interest in giving false testimony.

The credibility of a witness, then, should only diminish in proportion to the hatred, friendship, or connections, subsisting between him and the delinquent. One witness is not sufficient for, whilst the accused denies what the other affirms, truth remains suspended, and the right that every one has to be believed innocent turns the balance in his favour.

The credibility of a witness is the less as the atrociousness of the crime is greater, from the improbability of its having been committed; as in cases of witchcraft, and acts of wanton cruelty. The writers on penal laws have adopted a contrary principle, viz. that the credibility of a witness is greater as the crime is more atrocious. Behold their inhuman maxim, dictated by the most cruel imbecility. In atrocissimis, leviores conjecturae sufficiunt, licit judici jura transgredi. Let us translate this sentence, that mankind may see one of the many unreasonable principles to which they are ignorantly subject. In the most atrocious crimes, the slightest conjectures are sufficient, and the judge is allowed to exceed the limits of the law. The absurd practices of legislators are often the effect of timidity, which is a principal source of the contradictions of mankind. The legislators, (or rather lawyers, whose opinions when alive were interested and venal, but which after their death become of decisive authority, and are the sovereign arbiters of the lives and fortunes of men), terrified by the condemnation of some innocent person, have burdened the law with pompous and useless formalities, the scrupulous observance of which will place anarchical impunity on the throne of justice; at other times, perplexed by atrocious crimes of difficult proof, they imagined themselves under a necessity of superseding the very formalities established by themselves; and thus, at one time with despotic impatience, and at another with feminine timidity, they transform their solemn judgments into a game of hazard.

But, to return: in the case of witchcraft, it is much more probable that a number of men should be deceived than that any person should exercise a power which God hath refused to every created being. In like manner, in cases of wanton cruelty, the presumption is always against the accuser; for no man is cruel without some interest, without some motive of fear or hate. There are no spontaneous or superfluous sentiments in the heart of man; they are all the result of impressions on the senses.

The credibility of a witness may also be diminished by his being a member of a private society, whose customs and principles of conduct are either not known or are different from those of the public.

Such a man has not only his own passions, but those of the society of which he is a member.

Finally, the credibility of a witness is still when the question relates to the words of a criminal; for the tone of voice, the gesture, all that precedes, accompanies, and follows the different ideas which men annex to the same words, may so alter and modify a man's discourse, that it is almost impossible to repeat them precisely in the manner in which they were spoken. Besides, violent and uncommon actions, such as real crimes, leave a trace in the multitude of circumstances that attend them, and in their effects; but words remain only in the memory of the hearers, who are commonly negligent or prejudiced. It is infinitely easier, then, to found an accusation on the words than an the actions of a man; for in these the number of circumstances urged against the accused afford him variety of means of justification.

Of Evidence and the Proofs of a Crime, and of the Form of Judgment

***

The following general theorem is of great use determining the certainty of a fact. When the proofs of a crime are dependent on each other, that is, when the evidence of each witness, taken separately, proves nothing, or when all the proofs are dependent upon one, the number of proofs neither increase nor diminish the probability of the fact; foe the force of the whole is no greater than the force of that on which they depend, and if this fails, they all fall to the ground. When the proofs are independent on each other, the probability of the fact increases in proportion to the number of proofs; for the falsehood of the one does not diminish the veracity of another.

It may seem extraordinary that I speak of probability with regard to crimes, which to deserve a punishment, must be certain. But this paradox will vanish when it is considered, that, strictly speaking, moral certainty is only probability, but which is called a certainty, because every man in his senses assents to it from an habit produced by the necessity of acting, and which is anterior to all speculation. That certainty which is necessary to decide that the accused is guilty is the very same which determines every man in the most important transactions of his life.

The proofs of a crime may be divided into two classes, perfect and imperfect. I call those perfect which exclude the possibility of innocence; imperfect, those which do not exclude this possibility. Of the first, one only is sufficient for condemnation; of the second, as many are required as form a perfect proof; that is to say, that though each of these, separately taken, does not exclude the possibility of innocence, it is nevertheless excluded by their union. It should be also observed, that the imperfect proofs, of which the accused, if innocent, might clear himself, and does not become perfect.

But it is much easier to feel this moral certainty of proofs than to define it exactly. For this reason, I think it an excellent law which establishes assistants to the principal judge, and those chosen by lot; for that ignorance which judges by its feelings is less subject to error than the knowledge or the laws which judges by opinion. Where the laws are clear and precise, the office of the judge is merely to ascertain the fact. If, in examining the proofs of a crime, acuteness and dexterity be required, if clearness and precision be necessary in summoning up the result, to judge of the result itself nothing is wanting but plain and ordinary good sense, a less fallacious guide than the knowledge, of a judge, accustomed to find guilty, and to reduce all things to an artificial system borrowed from his studies. Happy the nation where the knowledge of the law is not a science!

It is an admirable law which ordains that every man shall be tried by his peers; for, when life, liberty and fortune, are in question, the sentiments which a difference of rank and fortune inspires should be silent; that superiority with which the fortunate look upon the unfortunate, and that envy with which the inferior regard their superiors, should have no influence. But when the crime is an offence against a fellow-subject, one half of the judges should be peers to the accused, and the other peers to the person offended: so that all private interest, which, in spite of ourselves, modifies the appearance of objects, even in the eyes of the most equitable, is counteracted, and nothing remains to turn aside the direction of truth and the laws. It is also just that the accused should have the liberty of excluding a certain number of his judges; where this liberty is, enjoyed for a long time, without any instance to the contrary, the criminal seems to condemn himself.

All trials should be public, that opinion, which is the best, or perhaps the only cement of society, may curb the authority of the powerful, and the passions of the judge, and that the people may say, “We are protected by the laws; we are not slaves”; a sentiment which inspires courage, and which is the best tribute to a sovereign who knows his real interest. I shall not enter into particulars. There may be some persons who expect that I should say all that can be said upon this subject; to such what I have already written must be unintelligible.

Of secret Accusations

***

Secret accusations are a manifest abuse, but consecrated by custom in many nations, where, from the weakness of the government, they are necessary. This custom makes men false and treacherous. Whoever suspects another to be an informer, beholds in him an enemy; and from thence mankind are accustomed to disguise their real sentiments; and, from the habit of concealing them from others, they at last even hide them from themselves. Unhappy are those who have arrived at this point! without any certain and fixed principles to guide them, they fluctuate in the vast sea of opinion, and are busied only in escaping the monsters which surround them: to those the present is always embittered by the uncertainty of the future; deprived of the pleasures of tranquillity and security, some fleeting moments of happiness, scattered thinly through their wretched lives, console them for the misery of existing. Shall we, amongst such men, find intrepid soldiers, to defend their king and country? Amongst such men shall we find incorruptible magistrates, who, with the spirit of freedom and patriotic eloquence, will support and explain the true interest of their sovereign; who, with the tributes, offer up at the throne the love and blessing of the people, and thus bestow on the palaces of the great and the humble cottage peace and security, and to the industrious a prospect of bettering their lot that useful ferment and vital principle of states?

Who can defend himself from calumny, armed with that impenetrable shield of tyranny, secrecy? What a miserable government must that be where the sovereign suspects an enemy in every subject, and, to secure the tranquillity of the public, is obliged to sacrifice the repose of every individual.

By what argument is it pretended that secret accusations may be justified? The public safety, say they, and the security and maintenance of the established form of government. But what a strange constitution is that where the government which hath in its favour not only power, but opinion, still more efficacious, yet fears its own subjects? The indemnity of the informer; do not the laws defend him sufficiently? and are there subjects more powerful than the laws? The necessity of protecting the informer from infamy; then secret calumny is authorised, and punished only when public. The nature of the crime; if actions, indifferent in themselves, or even useful to the public, were called crimes, both the accusation and the trial could never be too secret. But can there be any crime committed against the public which ought not to be publicly punished? I respect all governments; and I speak not of any one in particular. Such may sometimes be the nature of circumstances, that, when abuses are inherent in the constitution, it may be imagined, that to rectify them would be to destroy the constitution itself. But, were I to dictate new laws in a remote corner of the universe, the good of posterity, ever present to my mind, would hold back my trembling hand, and prevent me from authorising secret accusations.

Public accusations, says Montesquieu, are more conformable to the nature of a republic, where zeal for the public good is the principal passion of a citizen, than of a monarchy, in which, as this sentiment is very feeble, from the nature of the government, the best establishment is that of commissioners, who, in the name of the public, accuse the infractors of the laws. But in all governments, as well in a republic as in a monarchy, the punishment due to the crime of which one accuses another ought to be inflicted on the informer.

Of Torture

***

The torture of a criminal during the course of his trial is a cruelty consecrated by custom in most nations. It is used with an intent either to make him confess his crime, or to explain some contradictions into which he had been led during his examination, or discover his accomplices, or for some kind of metaphysical and incomprehensible purgation of infamy, or, finally, in order to discover other crimes of which he is not accused, but of which he may be guilty.

No man can be judged a criminal until he be found guilty; nor can society take from him the public protection until it have been proved that he has violated the conditions on which it was granted. What right, then, but that of power, can authorise the punishment of a citizen so long as there remains any doubt of his guilt? This dilemma is frequent. Either he is guilty, or not guilty. If guilty, he should only suffer the punishment ordained by the laws, and torture becomes useless, as his confession is unnecessary, if he be not guilty, you torture the innocent; for, in the eye of the law, every man is innocent whose crime has not been proved. Besides, it is confounding all relations to expect that a man should be both the accuser and accused; and that pain should be the test of truth, as if truth resided in the muscles and fibres of a wretch in torture. By this method the robust will escape, and the feeble be condemned. These are the inconveniences of this pretended test of truth, worthy only of a cannibal, and which the Romans, in many respects barbarous, and whose savage virtue has been too much admired, reserved for the slaves alone.

What is the political intention of punishments? To terrify and be an example to others. Is this intention answered by thus privately torturing the guilty and the innocent? It is doubtless of importance that no crime should remain unpunished; but it is useless to make a public example of the author of a crime hid in darkness. A crime already committed, and for which there can be no remedy, can only be punished by a political society with an intention that no hopes of impunity should induce others to commit the same. If it be true, that the number of those who from fear or virtue respect the laws is greater than of those by whom they are violated, the risk of torturing an innocent person is greater, as there is a greater probability that, cæteris paribus, an individual hath observed, than that he hath infringed the laws.

There is another ridiculous motive for torture, namely, to purge a man from infamy. Ought such an abuse to be tolerated in the eighteenth century? Can pain, which is a sensation, have any connection with a moral sentiment, a matter of opinion? Perhaps the rack may be considered as the refiner's furnace.

It is not difficult to trace this senseless law to its origin; for an absurdity, adopted by a whole nation, must have some affinity with other ideas established and respected by the same nation. This custom seems to be the offspring of religion, by which mankind, in all nations and in all ages, are so generally influenced. We are taught by our infallible church, that those stains of sin contracted through human frailty, and which have not deserved the eternal anger of the Almighty, are to be purged away in another life by an incomprehensible fire. Now infamy is a stain, and if the punishments and fire of purgatory can take away all spiritual stains, why should not the pain of torture take away those of a civil nature? I imagine, that the confession of a criminal, which in some tribunals is required as being essential to his condemnation, has a similar origin, and has been taken from the mysterious tribunal of penitence, were the confession of sins is a necessary part of the sacrament. Thus have men abused the unerring light of revelation; and, in the times of tractable ignorance, having no other, they naturally had recourse to it on every occasion, making the most remote and absurd applications. Moreover, infamy is a sentiment regulated neither by the laws nor by reason, but entirely by opinion; but torture renders the victim infamous, and therefore cannot take infamy away.

Another intention of torture is to oblige the supposed criminal to reconcile the contradictions into which he may have fallen during his examination; as if the dread of punishment, the uncertainty of his fate, the solemnity of the court, the majesty of the judge, and the ignorance of the accused, were not abundantly sufficient to account for contradictions, which are so common to men even in a state of tranquillity, and which must necessarily be multiplied by the perturbation of the mind of a man entirely engaged in the thoughts of saving himself from imminent danger.

This infamous test of truth is a remaining monument of that ancient and savage legislation, in which trials by fire, by boiling water, or the uncertainty of combats, were called judgments of God; as if the links of that eternal chain, whose beginning is in the breast of the first cause of all things, could ever be disunited by the institutions of men. The only difference between torture and trials by fire and boiling water is, that the event of the first depends on the will of the accused, and of the second on a fact entirely physical and external: but this difference is apparent only, not real. A man on the rack, in the convulsions of torture, has it as little in his power to declare the truth, as, in former times, to prevent without fraud the effects of fire or boiling water.

Every act of the will is invariably in proportion to the force of the impression on our senses. The impression of pain, then, may increase to such a degree, that, occupying the mind entirely, it will compel the sufferer to use the shortest method of freeing himself from torment. His answer, therefore, will be an effect as necessary as that of fire or boiling water, and he will accuse himself of crimes of which he is innocent: so that the very means employed to distinguish the innocent from the guilty will most effectually destroy all difference between them.

It would be superfluous to confirm these reflections by examples of innocent persons who, from the agony of torture, have confessed themselves guilty: innumerable instances may be found in all nations, and in every age. How amazing that mankind have always neglected to draw the natural conclusion! Lives there a man who, if he has carried his thoughts ever so little beyond the necessities of life, when he reflects on such cruelty, is not tempted to fly from society, and return to his natural state of independence?

The result of torture, then, is a matter of calculation, and depends on the constitution, which differs in every individual, and it is in proportion to his strength and sensibility; so that to discover truth by this method, is a problem which may be better solved by a mathematician than by a judge, and may be thus stated: The force of the muscles and the sensibility of the nerves of an innocent person being given, it is required to find the degree of pain necessary to make him confess himself guilty of a given crime.

The examination of the accused is intended to find out the truth; but if this be discovered with so much difficulty in the air, gesture, and countenance of a man at case, how can it appear in a countenance distorted by the convulsions of torture? Every violent action destroys those small alterations in the features which sometimes disclose the sentiments of the heart.

These truths were known to the Roman legislators, amongst whom, as I have already observed, slaves only, who were not considered as citizens, were tortured. They are known to the English a nation in which the progress of science, superiority in commerce, riches, and power, its natural consequences, together with the numerous examples of virtue and courage, leave no doubt of the excellence of its laws. They have been acknowledged in Sweden, where torture has been abolished. They are known to one of the wisest monarchs in Europe, who, having seated philosophy on the throne by his beneficent legislation, has made his subjects free, though dependent on the laws; the only freedom that reasonable men can desire in the present state of things. In short, torture has not been thought necessary in the laws of armies, composed chiefly of the dregs of mankind, where its use should seem most necessary. Strange phenomenon! that a set of men, hardened by slaughter, and familiar with blood, should teach humanity to the sons of peace.

It appears also that these truths were known, though imperfectly, even to those by whom torture has been most frequently practised; for a confession made during torture, is null, if it be not afterwards confirmed by an oath, which if the criminal refuses, he is tortured again. Some civilians and some nations permit this infamous petitio principii to be only three times repeated, and others leave it to the discretion of the judge; therefore, of two men equally innocent, or equally guilty, the most robust and resolute will be acquitted, and the weakest and most pusillanimous will be condemned, in consequence of the following excellent mode of reasoning. I, the judge, must find some one guilty. Thou, who art a strong fellow, hast been able to resist the force of torment; therefore I acquit thee. Thou, being weaker, hast yielded to it; I therefore condemn thee. I am sensible, that the confession which was extorted from thee has no weight; but if thou dost not confirm by oath what thou hast already confessed, I will have thee tormented again.

A very strange but necessary consequence of the use of torture is, that the case of the innocent is worse than that of the guilty. With regard to the first, either he confesses the crime which he has not committed, and is condemned, or he is acquitted, and has suffered a punishment he did not deserve. On the contrary, the person who is really guilty has the most favourable side of the question; for, if he supports the torture with firmness and resolution, he is acquitted, and has gained, having exchanged a greater punishment for a less.

The law by which torture is authorised, says, Men, be insensible to pain. Nature has indeed given you an irresistible self-love, and an unalienable right of self-preservation; but I create in you a contrary sentiment, an heroic hatred of yourselves. I command you to accuse yourselves, and to declare the truth, amidst the tearing of your flesh, and the dislocation of your bones.

Torture is used to discover whether the criminal be guilty of other crimes besides those of which he is accused, which is equivalent to the following reasoning. Thou art guilty of one crime, therefore it is possible that thou mayest have committed a thousand others; but the affair being doubtful I must try it by my criterion of truth. The laws order thee to be tormented because thou art guilty, because thou mayest be guilty, and because I choose thou shouldst be guilty.

Torture is used to make the criminal discover his accomplices; but if it has been demonstrated that it is not at a proper means of discovering truth, how can it serve to discover the accomplices, which is one of the truths required? Will not the man who accuses himself yet more readily accuse others? Besides, is it just to torment one man for the crime of another? May not the accomplices be found out by the examination of the witnesses, or of the criminal; from the evidence, or from the nature of the crime itself; in short, by all the means that have been used to prove the guilt of the prisoner? The accomplices commonly fly when their comrade is taken. The uncertainty of their fate condemns them to perpetual exile, and frees society from the danger of further injury; whilst the punishment of the criminal, by deterring others, answers the purpose for which it was ordained.

Of pecuniary Punishments

***

There was a time when all punishments were pecuniary. The crimes of the subjects were the inheritance of the prince. An injury done to society was a favour to the crown; and the sovereign and magistrates, those guardians of the public security, were interested in the violation of the laws. Crimes were tried, at that time, in a court of exchequer, and the cause became a civil suit between the person accused and the crown. The magistrate then had other powers than were necessary for the public welfare, and the criminal suffered other punishments than the necessity of example required. The judge was rather a collector for the crown, an agent for the treasury, than a protector and minister of the laws. But according to this system, for a man to confess himself guilty was to acknowledge himself a debtor to the crown; which was, and is at present (the effects continuing after the causes have ceased) the intent of all criminal causes. Thus, the criminal who refuses to confess his crime, though convicted by the most undoubted proofs, will suffer a less punishment than if he had confessed; and he will not be put to the torture to oblige him to confess other crimes which he might have committed, as he has not confessed the principal. But the confession being once obtained, the judge becomes master of his body, and torments him with a studied formality, in order to squeeze out of him all the profit possible. Confession, then, is allowed to be a convincing proof, especially when obtained by the force of torture; at the same time that an extrajudicial confession, when a man is at ease and under no apprehension, is not sufficient for his condemnation.

All inquiries which may serve to clear up the fact, but which may weaken the pretensions of the crown, are excluded. It was not from compassion to the criminal, or from considerations of humanity, that torments were sometimes spared, but out of fear of losing those rights which at present appear chimerical and inconceivable. The judge becomes an enemy to the accused, to a wretch a prey to the horrors of a dungeon, to torture, to death, and an uncertain futurity, more terrible than all; he inquires not into the truth of the fact, but the nature of the crime; he lays snares to make him convict himself; he fears lest he should not succeed in finding him guilty, and lest that infallibility which every man arrogates to himself should be called in question. It is in the power of the magistrate to determine what evidence is sufficient to send a man to prison; that he may be proved innocent, he must first be supposed guilty. This is what is called an offensive prosecution; and such are all criminal proceedings in the eighteenth century, in all parts of our polished Europe. The true prosecution, for information, that is, an impartial inquiry into the fact, that which reason prescribes, which military laws adopt, and which Asiatic despotism allows in suits of one subject against another, is very little practised in any courts of justice. What a labyrinth of absurdities! Absurdities which will appear increditable to happier posterity. The philosopher only will be able to read, in the nature of man, the possibility of there ever having been such a system.

Of Oaths

***

There is a palpable contradiction between the laws and the natural sentiments of mankind in the case of oaths, which are administered to a criminal to make him speak the truth, when the contrary is his greatest interest; as if a man could think himself obliged to contribute to his own destruction, and as if, when interest speaks, religion was not generally silent, religion, which in all ages hath, of all other things, been most commonly abused: and indeed, upon what motive should it be respected by the wicked, when it has been thus violated by those who were esteemed the wisest of men? The motives which religion opposes to the fear of impending evil and the love of life are too weak, as they are too distant, to make any impression on the senses. The affairs of the other world are regulated by laws entirely different from those by which human affairs are directed; why then should you endeavour to compromise matters between them? Why should a man be reduced to the terrible alternative, either of offending God, or of contributing to his own immediate destruction? The laws which require an oath in such a case leave him only the choice of becoming a bad Christian or a martyr. For this reason, oaths become, by degrees, a mere formality, and all sentiments of religion, perhaps the only motive of honesty in the greatest part of mankind, are destroyed. Experience proves their inutility: I appeal to every judge, whether he has ever known that an oath alone has brought truth from the lips of a criminal; and reason tells us, it must be so; for all laws are useless, and in consequence destructive, which contradict the natural feelings of mankind. Such laws are like a dike, opposed directly to the course of a torrent; it is either immediately overwhelmed, or, by a whirlpool formed by itself, it is gradually undermined and destroyed.

Of the Advantage of immediate Punishment

***

The more immediately after the commission of a crime a punishment is inflicted, the more just and useful it will be. It will be more just, because it spares the criminal the cruel and superfluous torment of uncertainty, which increases in proportion to the strength of his imagination and the sense of his weakness; and because the privation of liberty, being a punishment, ought to be inflicted before condemnation but for as short a time as possible. Imprisonment, I say, being only the means of securing the person of the accused until be be tried, condemned, or acquitted, ought not only to be of as short duration, but attended with as little severity as possible. The time should be determined by the necessary preparation for the trial, and the right of priority in the oldest prisoners. The confinement ought not to be closer than is requisite to prevent his flight, or his concealing the proofs of the crime; and the trial should be conducted with all possible expedition. Can there be a more cruel contrast than that between the indolence of a judge and the painful anxiety of the accused; the comforts and pleasures of an insensible magistrate, and the filth and misery of the prisoner? In general, as I have before observed, The degree of the punishment, and the consequences of a crime, ought to be so contrived as to have the greatest possible effect on others, with the least possible pain to the delinquent. If there be any society in which this is not a fundamental principle, it is an unlawful society; for mankind, by their union, originally intended to subject themselves to the least evils possible.

An immediate punishment is more useful; because the smaller the interval of time between the punishment and the crime, the stronger and more lasting will be the association of the two ideas of crime and punishment; so that they may be considered, one as the cause, and the other as the unavoidable and necessary effect. It is demonstrated, that the association of ideas is the cement which unites the fabric of the human intellect, without which pleasure and pain would be simple and ineffectual sensations. The vulgar, that is, all men who have no general ideas or universal principles, act in consequence of the most immediate and familiar associations; but the more remote and complex only present themselves to the minds of those who are passionately attached to a single object, or to those of greater understanding, who have acquired an habit of rapidly comparing together a number of objects, and of forming a conclusion; and the result, that is, the action in consequence, by these means becomes less dangerous and uncertain.

It is, then, of the. greatest importance that the punishment should succeed the crime as immediately as possible, if we intend that, in the rude minds of the multitude, the seducing picture of the advantage arising from the crime should instantly awake the attendant idea of punishment. Delaying the punishment serves only to separate these two ideas, and thus affects the minds of the spectators rather as being a terrible sight than the necessary consequence of a crime, the horror of which should contribute to heighten the idea of the punishment.

There is another excellent method of strengthening this important connection between the ideas of crime and punishment; that is, to make the punishment as analogous as possible to the nature of the crime, in order that the punishment may lead the mind to consider the crime in a different point of view from that in which it was placed by the flattering idea of promised advantages.

Crimes of less importance are commonly punished either in the obscurity of a prison, or the criminal is transported, to give by his slavery an example to societies which he never offended; an example absolutely useless, because distant from the place where the crime was committed. Men do not, in general, commit great crimes deliberately, but rather in a sudden gust of passion; and they commonly look on the punishment due to a great crime as remote and improbable. The public punishment, therefore, of small crimes will make a greater impression, and, by deterring men from the smaller, will effectually prevent the greater.

Of Acts of violence

***

Some crimes relate to person, others to property. The first ought to be punished corporally. The great and rich should by no means have it in their power to set a price on the security of the weak and indigent; for then riches, which, under the protection of the laws, are the reward of industry, would become the aliment of tyranny. Liberty is at an end whenever the laws permit that, in certain cases, a man may cease to be a person, and become a thing. Then will the powerful employ their address to select from the various combinations of civil society all that is in their own favour. This is that magic art which transforms subjects into beasts of burden, and which, in the hands of the strong, is the chain that binds the weak and incautious. Thus it is that in some governments, where there is all the appearance of Liberty, tyranny lies concealed, and insinuates itself into some neglected corner of the constitution, where it gathers strength insensibly. Mankind generally oppose, with resolution, the assaults of barefaced and open tyranny, but disregard the little insect that gnaws through the dike, and opens a sure though secret passage to inundation.

Of the Punishment of the Nobles

***

What punishments shall be ordained for the nobles, whose privileges make so great a part of the laws of nations? I do not mean to inquire whether the hereditary distinction between nobles and commoners be useful in any government, or necessary in a monarchy; or whether it be true that they form an intermediate power, of use in moderating the excess of both extremes; or whether they be not rather slaves to to their own body, and to others, confining within a very small circle the natural effects and hopes of industry, like those little fruitful spots scattered here and there in the sandy deserts of Arabia; or whether it be true that a subordination of rank and condition is inevitable or useful in society; and, if so, whether this subordination should not rather subsist between individuals than particular bodies, whether it should not rather circulate through the whole body politic than be confined to one part, and, rather than be perpetual, should it not be incessantly produced and destroyed. Be these as they may, I assert that the punishment of a nobleman should in no wise differ from that of the lowest member of society.

Every lawful distinction, either in honours or riches, supposes previous equality, founded on the laws, on which all the members of society are considered as being equally dependent. We should suppose that men, in renouncing their natural despotism, said, The wisest and most industrious among us should obtain the greatest honours, and his dignity shall descend to his posterity. The fortunate and happy may hope for greater honours, but let him not therefore be less afraid than others of violating those conditions on which he is exalted. It is true indeed that no such degrees were ever made in a general diet of mankind, but they exist in the invariable relations of things; nor do they destroy the advantages which are supposed to be produced by the class of nobles, but prevent the inconveniences; and they make the laws respectable, by destroying all hopes of impunity.

It may be objected, that the same punishment inflicted on a nobleman and a plebeian becomes really different from the difference of their education, and from the infamy it reflects on an illustrious family: but I answer, that punishments are to be estimated, not by the sensibility of the criminal, but by the injury done to society, which injury is augmented by the high rank of the offender. The precise equality of a punishment can never be more than external, as it is in proportion to the degree of sensibility which differs in every individual. The infamy of an innocent family may be easily obliterated by some public demonstration of favour from the sovereign, and forms have always more influence than reason on the gazing multitude.

Of the Punishment of the Nobles

***

What punishments shall be ordained for the nobles, whose privileges make so great a part of the laws of nations? I do not mean to inquire whether the hereditary distinction between nobles and commoners be useful in any government, or necessary in a monarchy; or whether it be true that they form an intermediate power, of use in moderating the excess of both extremes; or whether they be not rather slaves to to their own body, and to others, confining within a very small circle the natural effects and hopes of industry, like those little fruitful spots scattered here and there in the sandy deserts of Arabia; or whether it be true that a subordination of rank and condition is inevitable or useful in society; and, if so, whether this subordination should not rather subsist between individuals than particular bodies, whether it should not rather circulate through the whole body politic than be confined to one part, and, rather than be perpetual, should it not be incessantly produced and destroyed. Be these as they may, I assert that the punishment of a nobleman should in no wise differ from that of the lowest member of society.

Every lawful distinction, either in honours or riches, supposes previous equality, founded on the laws, on which all the members of society are considered as being equally dependent. We should suppose that men, in renouncing their natural despotism, said, The wisest and most industrious among us should obtain the greatest honours, and his dignity shall descend to his posterity. The fortunate and happy may hope for greater honours, but let him not therefore be less afraid than others of violating those conditions on which he is exalted. It is true indeed that no such degrees were ever made in a general diet of mankind, but they exist in the invariable relations of things; nor do they destroy the advantages which are supposed to be produced by the class of nobles, but prevent the inconveniences; and they make the laws respectable, by destroying all hopes of impunity.

It may be objected, that the same punishment inflicted on a nobleman and a plebeian becomes really different from the difference of their education, and from the infamy it reflects on an illustrious family: but I answer, that punishments are to be estimated, not by the sensibility of the criminal, but by the injury done to society, which injury is augmented by the high rank of the offender. The precise equality of a punishment can never be more than external, as it is in proportion to the degree of sensibility which differs in every individual. The infamy of an innocent family may be easily obliterated by some public demonstration of favour from the sovereign, and forms have always more influence than reason on the gazing multitude.

Of Robbery

***

The punishment of robbery, not accompanied with violence, should be pecuniary. He who endeavours to enrich himself with the property of another should be deprived of part of his own. But this crime, alas! is commonly the effect of misery and despair; the crime of that unhappy part of mankind to whom the right of exclusive property, a terrible and perhaps unnecessary right, has left but a bare existence. Besides, as pecuniary punishments may increase the number of robbers, by increasing the number of poor, and may deprive an innocent family of subsistence, the most proper punishment will be that kind of slavery which alone can be called just; that is, which makes the society, for a time, absolute master of the person and labour of the criminal, in order to oblige him to repair, by this dependence, the unjust despotism he usurped over the property of another, and his violation of the social compact.

When robbery is attended with violence, corporal punishment should be added to slavery. Many writers have shown the evident disorder which must arise from not distinguishing the punishment due to robbery with violence, and that due to theft or robbery committed with dexterity, absurdly making a sum of money equivalent to a man's life. But it can never be superfluous to repeat, again and again, those truths of which mankind have not profited; for political machines preserve their motion much longer than others, and receive a new impulse with more difficulty. These crimes are in their nature absolutely different, and this axiom is as certain in politics as in mathematics, that between qualities of different natures there can be no similitude.

Of Infamy considered as a Punishment

***

Those injuries which affect the honour, that is, that just portion of esteem which every citizen has a right to expect from others, should be punished with infamy. Infamy is a mark of the public disapprobation, which, deprives the object of all consideration in the eyes of his fellow-citizens, of the confidence of his country, and of that fraternity which exists between members of the same society. This is not always in the power of the laws. It is necessary that the infamy inflicted by the laws should be the same with that which results from the relations of things, from universal morality, or from that particular system, adopted by the nation, and the laws, which governs the opinion of the vulgar. If, on the contrary, one be different from the other, either the laws will no longer be respected, or the received notions of morality and probity will vanish, in spite of the declamations of moralists, which are always too weak to resist the force of example. If we declare those actions infamous which are in themselves indifferent. we lessen the infamy of those which are really infamous. The punishment of infamy should not be too frequent, for the power of opinion grows weaker by repetition; nor should it be inflicted on a number of persons at the same time, for the infamy of many resolves itself into the infamy of none.

Painful and corporal punishments should never be applied to fanaticism; for, being founded on pride, it glories in persecution. Infamy and ridicule only should be employed against fanatics if the first, their pride will be overbalanced by the pride of the people; and we may judge of the power of the second, if we consider that even truth Is obliged to summon all her force when attacked by error armed with ridicule. Thus, by opposing one passion to another, and opinion to opinion, a wise legislator puts an end to the admiration of the populace occasioned by a false principle, the original absurdity of which is veiled by some well deduced consequences.

This is the method to avoid confounding the immutable relations of things, or opposing nature, whose actions, not being limited by time, but operating incessantly, overturn and destroy all those vain regulations which contradict her laws. It is not only in the fine arts that the imitation of nature is the fundamental principle; it is the same

in sound policy, which is no other than the art of uniting and directing to the same end the natural and immutable sentiments of mankind.

Of Idleness

***

A wise government will not suffer in the midst of labour and industry, that kind of political idleness which is confounded by rigid declaimers with the leisure attending riches acquired by industry, which is of use to an increasing society when confined within proper limits. I call those politically idle, who neither contribute to the good of society by their labour nor their riches; who continually accumulate, but never spend; who are reverenced by the vulgar with stupid admiration, and regarded by the wise with disdain; who, being victims to a monastic life, and deprived of all incitement to that activity which is necessary to preserve or increase its comforts, devote all their vigour to passions of the strongest kind, the passions of opinion. I call not him idle who enjoys the fruits of the virtues or vices of his ancestors, and, in exchange for his pleasures, supports the industrious poor. It is not then the narrow virtue of austere moralists, but the laws, that should determine what species of idleness deserves punishment.

Of Banishment and Confiscation

***

He who disturbs the public tranquillity, who does not obey the laws, who violates the conditions on which men mutually support and defend each other, ought to be excluded from society, that is, banished.

It seems as if banishment should be the punishment of those who, being accused of an atrocious crime, are probably, but not certainly, guilty. For this purpose would be required a law the least arbitrary and the most precise possible; which should condemn to banishment those who have reduced the community to the fatal alternative either of fearing or punishing them unjustly, still, however, leaving them the sacred right of proving their innocence. The reasons ought to be stronger for banishing a citizen than a stranger, and for the first accusation than for one who hath been often accused.

Should the person who is excluded for ever from society be deprived of his property? This question may be considered in different lights. The confiscation of effects, added to banishment is a greater punishment than banishment alone; there ought then to be some cases, in which, according to the crime, either the whole fortune should be confiscated, or part only, or none at all. The whole should be forfeited, when the law which ordains banishment declares, at the same time, that all connections or relations between the society and the criminal are annihilated. In this case the citizen dies; the man only remains, and, with respect to a political body, the death of the citizen should have the same consequences with the death of the man. It seems to follow then, that in this case, the effects of the criminal should devolve to his lawful heirs. But it is not on account of this refinement that I disapprove of confiscations. If some have insisted, that they were a restraint to vengeance and the violence of particulars, they have not reflected, that, though punishments be productive of good, they are not, on that account, more just; to be just, they must be necessary. Even an useful injustice can never be allowed by a legislator, who means to guard against watchful tyranny, which, under the flattering pretext of momentary advantages, would establish permanent principles of destruction, and, to procure the ease of a few in a high station, would draw tears from thousands of the poor.

The law which ordains confiscations sets a price on the head of the subject, with the guilty punishes the innocent, and, by reducing them to indigence and despair, tempts them to become criminal. Can there be a more melancholy spectacle than a whole family overwhelmed with infamy and misery from the crime of their chief? a crime, which, if it had been possible, they were restrained from preventing, by that submission which the laws themselves have ordained.

Of the Spirit of Family in States

***

It is remarkable, that many fatal acts of injustice have been authorised and approved, even by the wisest and most experienced men, in the freest republics. This has been owing to their having considered the state rather as a society of families than of men. Let us suppose a nation composed of an hundred thousand men, divided into twenty thousand families of five persons each, including the head or master of the family, its representative. If it be an association of families, there will be twenty thousand men, and eighty thousand slaves; or if of men, there will be an hundred thousand citizens, and not one slave. In the first case we behold a republic, and twenty thousand little monarchies, of which the heads are the sovereigns: in the second the spirit of liberty will not only breath in every public place of the city, and in the assemblies of the nation, but in private houses, where men find the greatest part of their happiness or misery. As laws and customs are always the effect of the habitual sentiments of the members of a republic, if the society be an association of the heads of families, the spirit of monarchy will gradually make its way into the republic itself, as its effects will only be restrained by the opposite interests of each, and not by an universal spirit of liberty and equality. The private spirit of family is a spirit of minuteness, and confined to little concerns. Public spirit, on the contrary, is influenced by general principles, and from facts deduces general rules of utility to the greatest number.

In a republic of families, the children remain under the authority of the father as long as he lives, and are obliged to wait until his death for an existence dependent on the laws alone. Accustomed to kneel and tremble in their tender years, when their natural sentiments were less restrained by that caution, obtained by experience, which is called moderation, how should they resist those obstacles which vice always opposes to virtue in the languor and decline of age, when the despair of reaping the fruits is alone sufficient to damp the vigour of their resolutions?

In a republic, where every man is a citizen, family-subordination is not the effect of compulsion, but of contract; and the sons, disengaged from the natural dependence which the weakness of infancy and the necessity of education required, become free members of society, but remain subject to the head of the family for their own advantage, as in the great society.

In a republic of families, the young people, that is, the most numerous and most useful part of the nation, are at the discretion of their fathers: in a republic of men, they are attached to their parents by no other obligation than that sacred and inviolable one of mutual assistance, and of gratitude for the benefits they have received; a sentiment destroyed not so much by the wickedness of the human heart, as by a mistaken subjection prescribed by the laws.

These contradictions between the laws of families and the fundamental laws of a state are the source of many others between public and private morality, which produce a perpetual conflict in the mind. Domestic morality inspires submission and fear; the other courage and liberty. That instructs a man to confine his beneficence to a small number of persons, not of his own choice; this to extend it to all mankind. That commands a continual sacrifice of himself to a vain idol called the good of the family, which is often no real good to any one of those who compose it; this teaches him to consider his own advantage, without offending the laws, or excites him to sacrifice himself for the good of his country, by rewarding him beforehand with the fanaticism it inspires. Such contradictions are the reason that men neglect the pursuit of virtue, which they can hardly distinguish amidst the obscurity and confusion of natural and moral objects. How frequently are men, upon a retrospection of their actions, astonished to find themselves dishonest?

In proportion to the increase of society each member becomes a smaller part of the whole; and the republican spirit diminishes in the same proportion, if neglected by the laws. Political societies, like the human body, have their limits circumscribed, which they cannot exceed, without disturbing their economy. It seems as if the greatness of a state ought to be inversely as the sensibility and activity of the individuals; if, on the contrary, population and activity increase in the same proportion, the laws. will with difficulty prevent the crimes arising from the good they have produced. An overgrown republic can only be saved from despotism by subdividing it into a number of confederate republics. But how is this practicable? By a despotic dictator, who, with the courage of Sylla, has as much genius for building up as that Roman had for pulling down. If he be an ambitious man, his reward will be immortal glory? if a philosopher, the blessings of his fellow citizens will sufficiently console him for the loss of authority, though he should not be insensible to their ingratitude.

In proportion as the sentiments which unite us to the state grow weaker, those which attach us to the objects which more immediately surround us grow stronger; therefore, in the most despotic government, friendships are more durable, and domestic virtues (which are always of the lowest class) are the most common, or the only virtues, existing. Hence it appears how confined have been the views of the greatest number of legislators.

Of the Mildness of Punishments

***

The course of my ideas has carried me away from my subject, to the elucidation of which I now return. Crimes are more effectually prevented by the certainty than the severity of punishment. Hence in a magistrate the necessity of vigilance, and in a judge of implacability, which, that it may become an useful virtue, should be joined to a mild legislation. The certainty of a small punishment will make a stronger impression than the fear of one more severe, if attended with the hopes of escaping; for it is the nature of mankind to be terrified at the approach of the smallest inevitable evil, whilst hope, the best gift of Heaven hath the power of dispelling the apprehension of a greater, especially if supported by examples of impunity, which weakness or avarice too frequently afford.

If punishments be very severe, men are naturally led to the perpetration of other crimes, to avoid the punishment due to the first. The countries and times most notorious for severity of punishments were always those in which the most bloody and inhuman actions and the most atrocious crimes were committed; for the hand of the legislator and the assassin were directed by the same spirit of ferocity, which on the throne dictated laws of iron to slaves and savages, and in private instigated the subject to sacrifice one tyrant to make room for another.

In proportion as punishments become more cruel, the minds of men, as a fluid rises to the same height with that which surrounds it, grow hardened and insensible; and the force of the passions still continuing, in the space of an hundred years the wheel terrifies no more than formerly the prison. That a punishment may produce the effect required, it is sufficient that the evil it occasions should exceed the good expected from the crime, including in the calculation the certainty of the punishment, and the privation of the expected advantage. All severity beyond this is superfluous, and therefore tyrannical.

Men regulate their conduct by the repeated impression of evils they know, and not by those with which they are unacquainted. Let us, for example, suppose two nations, in one of which the greatest punishment is perpetual slavery, and in the other the wheel: I say, that both will inspire the same degree of terror, and that their can be no reasons for increasing the punishments of the first, which are not equally valid for augmenting those of the second to more lasting and more ingenious modes of tormenting, and so on to the most exquisite refinements of a science too well known to tyrants.

There are yet two other consequences of cruel punishments, which counteract the purpose of their institution, which was, to prevent crimes. The first arises from the impossibility of establishing an exact proportion between the crime and punishment; for though ingenious cruelty hath greatly multiplied the variety of torments, yet the human frame can suffer only to a certain degree, beyond which it is impossible to proceed, be the enormity of the crime ever so great. The second consequence is impunity. Human nature is limited no less in evil than in good. Excessive barbarity can never be more than temporary, it being impossible that it should be supported by a permanent system of legislation; for if the laws be too cruel, they must be altered, or anarchy and impunity will succeed.

Is it possible without shuddering with horror, to read in history of the barbarous and useless torments that were cooly invented and executed by men who were called sages? Who does not tremble at the thoughts of thousands of wretches, whom their misery, either caused or tolerated by the laws, which favoured the few and outraged the many, had forced in despair to return to a state of nature, or accused of impossible crimes, the fabric of ignorance and superstition, or guilty only of having been faithful to their own principles; who, I say, can, without horror, think of their being torn to pieces, with slow and studied barbarity, by men endowed with the same passions and the same feelings? A delightful spectacle to a fanatic multitude!

Of the Punishment of Death

***

The useless profusion of punishments, which has never made men better induces me to inquire, whether the punishment of death be really just or useful in a well governed state? What right, I ask, have men to cut the throats of their fellow-creatures? Certainly not that on which the sovereignty and laws are founded. The laws, as I have said before, are only the sum of the smallest portions of the private liberty of each individual, and represent the general will, which is the aggregate of that of each individual. Did any one ever give to others the right of taking away his life? Is it possible that, in the smallest portions of the liberty of each, sacrificed to the good of the public, can be contained the greatest of all good, life? If it were so, how shall it be reconciled to the maxim which tells us, that a man has no right to kill himself, which he certainly must have, if he could give it away to another?

But the punishment of death is not authorised by any right; for I have demonstrated that no such right exists. It is therefore a war of a whole nation against a citizen whose destruction they consider as necessary or useful to the general good. But if I can further demonstrate that it is neither necessary nor useful, I shall have gained the cause of humanity.

The death of a citizen cannot be necessary but in one case: when, though deprived of his liberty, he has such power and connections as may endanger the security of the nation; when his existence may produce a dangerous revolution in the established form of government. But, even in this case, it can only be necessary when a nation is on the verge of recovering or losing its liberty, or in times of absolute anarchy, when the disorders themselves hold the place of laws: but in a reign of tranquillity, in a form of government approved by the united wishes of the nation, in a state well fortified from enemies without and supported by strength within, and opinion, perhaps more efficacious, where all power is lodged in the hands of a true sovereign, where riches can purchase pleasures and not authority, there can be no necessity for taking away the life of a subject.

If the experience of all ages be not sufficient to prove, that the punishment of death has never prevented determined men from injuring society, if the example of the Romans, if twenty years' reign of Elizabeth, empress of Russia, in which she gave the fathers of their country an example more illustrious than many conquests bought with blood; if, I say, all this be not sufficient to persuade mankind, who always suspect the voice of reason, and who choose rather to be led by authority, let us consult human nature in proof of my assertion.

It is not the intenseness of the pain that has the greatest effect on the mind, but its continuance; for our sensibility is more easily and more powerfully affected by weak but repeated impressions, than by a violent but momentary impulse. The power of habit is universal over every sensible being. As it is by that we learn to speak, to walk, and to satisfy our necessities, so the ideas of morality are stamped on our minds by repeated impression. The death of a criminal is a terrible but momentary spectacle, and therefore a less efficacious method of deterring others than the continued example of a man deprived of his liberty, condemned, as a beast of burden, to repair, by his labour, the injury he has done to society, If I commit such a crime, says the spectator to himself, I shall be reduced to that miserable condition for the rest of my life. A much more powerful preventive than the fear of death which men always behold in distant obscurity.

The terrors of death make so slight an impression, that it has not force enough to withstand the forgetfulness natural to mankind, even in the most essential things, especially when assisted by the passions. Violent impressions surprise us, but their effect is momentary; they are fit to produce those revolutions which instantly transform a common man into a Lacedaemonian or a Persian; but in a free and quiet government they ought to be rather frequent than strong.

The execution of a criminal is to the multitude a spectacle which in some excites compassion mixed with indignation. These sentiments occupy the mind much more than that salutary terror which the laws endeavor to inspire; but, in the contemplation of continued suffering, terror is the only, or at least predominant sensation. The severity of a punishment should be just sufficient to excite compassion in the spectators, as it is intended more for them than for the criminal.

A punishment, to be just, should have only that degree of severity which is sufficient to deter others. Now there is no man whop upon the least reflection, would put in competition the total and perpetual loss of his liberty, with the greatest advantages he could possibly obtain in consequence of a crime. Perpetual slavery, then, has in it all that is necessary to deter the most hardened and determined, as much as the punishment of death. I say it has more. There are many who can look upon death with intrepidity and firmness, some through fanaticism, and others through vanity, which attends us even to the grave; others from a desperate resolution, either to get rid of their misery, or cease to live: but fanaticism and vanity forsake the criminal in slavery, in chains and fetters, in an iron cage, and despair seems rather the beginning than the end of their misery. The mind, by collecting itself and uniting all its force, can, for a moment, repel assailing grief; but its most vigorous efforts are insufficient to resist perpetual wretchedness.

In all nations, where death is used as a punishment, every example supposes a new crime committed; whereas, in perpetual slavery, every criminal affords a frequent and lasting example; and if it be necessary that men should often be witnesses of the power of the laws, criminals should often be put to death: but this supposes a frequency of crimes; and from hence this punishment will cease to have its effect, so that it must be useful and useless at the same time.

I shall be told that perpetual slavery is as painful a punishment as death, and therefore as cruel. I answer, that if all the miserable moments in the life of a slave were collected into one point, it would be a more cruel punishment than any other; but these are scattered through his whole life, whilst the pain of death exerts all its force in a moment. There is also another advantage in the punishment of slavery, which is, that it is more terrible to the spectator than to the sufferer himself; for the spectator considers the sum of all his wretched moments whilst the sufferer, by the misery of the present, is prevented from thinking of the future. All evils are increased by the imagination, and the sufferer finds resources and consolations of which the spectators are ignorant, who judge by their own sensibility of what passes in a mind by habit grown callous to misfortune.

Let us, for a moment, attend to the reasoning of a robber or assassin, who is deterred from violating the laws by the gibbet or the wheel. I am sensible, that to develop the sentiments of one's own heart is an art which education only can teach; but although a villain may not be able to give a clear account of his principles, they nevertheless influence his conduct. He reasons thus: “What are these laws that I am bound to respect, which make so great a difference between me and the rich man? He refuses me the farthing I ask of him, and excuses himself by bidding me have recourse to labour, with which he is unacquainted.”

“Who made these laws? The rich and the great, who never deigned to visit the miserable hut of the poor, who have never seen him dividing a piece of mouldy bread, amidst the cries of his famished children and the tears of his wife. Let us break those ties, fatal to the greatest part of mankind, and only useful to a few indolent tyrants. Let us attack injustice at its source. I will return to my natural state of independence. I shall live free and happy on the fruits of my courage and industry. A day of pain and repentance may come, but it will be short; and for an hour of grief I shall enjoy years of pleasure and liberty. King of a small number as determined as myself, I will correct the mistakes of fortune, and I shall see those tyrants grow pale and tremble at the sight of him, whom, with insulting pride, they would not suffer to rank with their dogs and horses."

Religion then presents itself to the mind of this lawless villain, and, promising him almost a certainty of eternal happiness upon the easy terms of repentance, contributes much to lessen the horror of the last scene of the tragedy.

But he who foresees that he must pass a great number of years, even his whole life, in pain and slavery, a slave to those laws by which he, was protected, in sight of his fellow-citizens, with whom he lives in freedom and society, makes an useful comparison between those evils, the uncertainty of his success, and the shortness of the time in which he shall enjoy the fruits of his transgression. The example of those wretches, continually before his eyes, makes a much greater impression on him than a punishment, which instead of correcting, makes him more obdurate.

The punishment of death is pernicious to society, from the example of barbarity it affords. If the passions, or the necessity of war, have taught men to shed the blood of their fellow creatures, the laws, which are intended to moderate the ferocity of mankind, should not increase it by examples of barbarity, the more horrible as this punishment is usually attended with formal pageantry. Is it not absurd, that the laws, which detest and punish homicide, should, in order to prevent murder, publicly commit murder themselves? What are the true and most useful laws? Those compacts and conditions which all would propose and observe in those moments when private interest is silent, or combined with that of the public. What are the natural sentiments of every person concerning the punishment of death? We may read them in the contempt and indignation with which every one looks on the executioner, who is nevertheless an innocent executor of the public will, a good citizen, who contributes to the advantage of society, the instrument of the general security within, as good soldiers are without. What then is the origin of this contradiction? Why is this sentiment of mankind indelible to the scandal of reason? It is, that, in a secret corner of the mind, in which the original impressions of nature are still preserved, men discover a sentiment which tells them, that their lives are not lawfully in the power of any one, but of that necessity only which with its iron sceptre rules the universe.

What must men think, when they see wise magistrates and grave ministers of justice, with indifference and tranquillity, dragging a criminal to death, and whilst a wretch trembles with agony, expecting the fatal stroke, the judge, who has condemned him, with the coldest insensibility, and perhaps with no small gratification from the exertion of his authority, quits his tribunal, to enjoy the comforts and pleasures of life? They will say, "Ah! those cruel formalities of justice are a cloak to tyranny, they are a secret language, a solemn veil, intended to conceal the sword by which we are sacrificed to the insatiable idol of despotism. Murder, which they would represent to us an horrible crime, we see practised by them without repugnance or remorse. Let us follow their example. A violent death appeared terrible in their descriptions, but we see that it is the affair of a moment. It will be still less terrible to him who, not expecting it, escapes almost all the pain." Such is the fatal though absurd reasonings of men who are disposed to commit crimes, on whom the abuse of religion has more influence than religion itself.

If it be objected, that almost all nations in all ages have punished certain crimes with death, I answer, that the force of these examples vanishes when opposed to truth, against which prescription is urged in vain. The history of mankind is an immense sea of errors, in which a few obscure truths may here and there be found.

But human sacrifices have also been common in almost all nations. That some societies only it either few in number, or for a very short time, abstained from the punishment of death, is rather favourable to my argument; for such is the fate of great truths, that their duration is only as a flash of lightning in the long and dark night of error. The happy time is not yet arrived, when truth, as falsehood has been hitherto, shall be the portion of the greatest number.

I am sensible that the voice of one philosopher is too weak to be heard amidst the clamours of a multitude, blindly influenced by custom; but there is a small number of sages scattered on the face of the earth, who will echo to me from the bottom of their hearts; and if these truths should happily force their way to the thrones of princes be it known to them, that they come attended with the secret wishes of all mankind; and tell the sovereign who deigns them a gracious reception, that his fame shall outshine the glory of conquerors, and that equitable posterity will exalt his peaceful trophies above those of a Titus, an Antoninus, or a Trajan.

How happy were mankind if laws were now to be first formed! now that we see on the thrones of Europe benevolent monarchs, friends to the virtues of peace, to the arts and sciences, fathers of their people, though crowned, yet citizens; the increase of whose authority augments the happiness of their subjects, by destroying that inter. mediate despotism which intercepts the prayers of the people to the throne. If these humane princes have suffered the old laws to subsist, it is doubtless because they are deterred by the numberless obstacles which oppose the subversion of errors established by the sanction of many ages; and therefore every wise citizen will wish for the increase of their authority.

Of imprisonment

***

That a magistrate, the executor of the laws, should have a power to imprison a citizen, to deprive the man he hates of his liberty, upon frivolous pretences, and to leave his friend unpunished, notwithstanding the strongest proofs of his guilt, is an error as common as it is contrary to the end of society, which is personal security.

Imprisonment is a punishment which differs from all others in this particular, that it necessarily precedes conviction; but this difference does not destroy a circumstance which is essential and common to it with all other punishments, viz. that it should never be inflicted but when ordained by the law. The law should therefore determine the crime, the presumption, and the evidence sufficient to subject the accused to imprisonment and examination. Public report, his flight, his extrajudicial confession, that of an accomplice, menaces, and his constant enmity with the person injured, the circumstances of the crime, and such other evidence, may be sufficient to justify the imprisonment of a citizen. But the nature of this evidence should be determined by the laws, and not by the magistrates, whose decrees are always contrary to political liberty, when they are not particular applications of a general maxim of the public code. When punishments become less severe, and prisons less horrible, when compassion and humanity shall penetrate the iron gates of dungeons, and direct the obdurate and inexorable ministers of justice, the laws may then be satisfied with weaker evidence for imprisonment.

A person accused, imprisoned, tried, and acquitted, ought not to be branded with any degree of infamy. Among the Romans we see that many accused of very great crimes, and afterwards declared innocent, were respected by the people, and honoured with employments in the state. But why is the fate of an innocent person so different in this age? It is because the present system of penal laws presents to our minds an idea of power rather than of justice: it is because the accused and convicted are thrown indiscriminately into the same prison? because imprisonment is rather a punishment than a means of securing the person of the accused; and because the interior power, which defends the laws, and the exterior, which defends the throne and kingdom, are separate, when they should be united. If the first were (under the common authority of the laws) combined with the right of judging, but not however immediately dependent on the magistrate, the pomp that attends a military corps would take off the infamy, which, like all popular opinions, is more attached to the manner and form than to the thing itself, as may be seen in military imprisonment, which, in the common opinion, is not so disgraceful as the civil. But the barbarity and ferocity of our ancestors, the hunters of the north, still subsist among the people in our customs and our laws, which are always several ages behind the actual refinements of a nation.

Of Prosecution and Prescription

***

The proofs of the crime being obtained, and the certainty of it determined, it is necessary to allow the criminal time and means for his justification; but a time so short as not to diminish that promptitude of punishment, which, as we have shewn, is one of the most powerful means of preventing crimes. A mistaken humanity may object to the shortness of the time, but the force of the objection will vanish if we consider that the danger of the innocent increases with the defects of the legislation.

The time for inquiry and for justification should be fixed by the laws, and not by the judge, who, in that case, would become legislator. With regard to atrocious crimes, which are long remembered, when they are once proved, if the criminal have fled, no time should be allowed; but in less considerable and more obscure crimes, a time should be fixed, after which the delinquent should be no longer uncertain of his fate: for, in the latter case, the length of time, in which the crime is almost forgotten, prevents the example of impunity, and allows the criminal to amend, and become a better member of society.

General principles will here be sufficient, it being impossible to fix precisely the limits of time for any given legislation, or for any society in any particular circumstance. I shall only add, that, in a nation willing to prove the utility of moderate punishment, laws which, according to the nature of the crime, increase or diminish the time of inquiry and justification, considering the imprisonment or the voluntary exile of the criminal as a part of the punishment, will form an easy division of a small number of mild punishments for a great number of crimes.

But it must be observed, the time for inquiry and justification should not increase in direct proportion to the atrociousness of crimes; for the probability of such crimes having been committed is inversely as their atrociousness. Therefore the time for inquiring ought, in some cases, to be diminished, and that for justification increased, et vice versa. This may appear to contradict what I have said above, namely, that equal punishments may be decreed by unequal crimes, by considering the time allowed the criminal or the prison as a punishment.

In order to explain this idea, I shall divide crimes into two classes. The first comprehends homicide, and all greater crimes; the second crimes of an inferior degree. This distinction is founded in human nature. The preservation of life is a natural right; the preservation of property is a right of society. The motives that induce men to shake off the natural sentiment of compassion, which must be destroyed before great crimes can be committed, are much less in number than those by which, from the natural desire of being happy, they are instigated to violate a right which is not founded in the heart of man, but is the work of society. The different degrees of probability in these two classes, require that they should be regulated on different principles. In the greatest crimes, as they are less frequent, and the probability of the innocence of the accused being greater, the time allowed him for his justification should be greater, and the time of inquiry less. For by hastening the definitive sentence, the flattering hopes of impunity are destroyed, which are more dangerous as the crime is more atrocious. On the contrary, in crimes of less importance, the probability of the innocence being less, the time of inquiry should be greater, and that of justification less, as impunity is not so dangerous.

But this division of crimes into two classes should not be admitted, if the consequences of impunity were in proportion to the probability of the crime. It should be considered, that a person accused, whose guilt or innocence is not determined for want of proofs, may be again imprisoned for the same crime, and be subject to a new trial, if fresh evidence arises within the time fixed.

This is, in my opinion, the best method of providing at the same time for the security and liberty of the subject, without favouring one at the expense of the other; which may easily happen, since both these blessings, the unalienable and equal patrimony of every citizen, are liable to be invaded, the one by open or disguised despotism, and the other by tumultuous and popular anarchy.

Of Crimes of difficult Proof

***

With the forgoing principles in view, it will appear astonishing, that reason hardly ever presided at the formation of the laws of nations that the weakest. and most equivocal evidence, and even conjectures, have been thought sufficient proof for crimes the most atrocious, (and therefore most improbable) the most obscure and chimerical; as if it were the interest of the laws and the judge not to enquire into the truth, but to prove the crime; as if there were not a greater risk of condemning an innocent person, when the probability of his guilt is less.

The generality of men want that vigour of mind and resolution which are as necessary for great crimes as for great virtues, and which at the same time produce both the one and the other in those nations. which are supported by the activity of their government, and a passion for the public good. For in those which subsist by their greatness or power, or by the goodness of their laws, the passions, being in a weaker degree, seem calculated rather to maintain than to improve the form of government. This naturally leads us to an important conclusion, viz. that great crimes do not always produce the destruction of a nation.

There are some crimes which, though frequent in society, are of difficult proof, a circumstance admitted as equal to the probability of the innocence of the accused. But as the frequency of these crimes is not owing to their impunity so much as to other causes, the danger of their passing unpunished is of less importance, and therefore the time of examination and prescription may be equally diminished. These principles are different from those commonly received; for it is in crimes which are proved with the greatest difficulty, such as adultery and sodomy, that presumptions, half proofs, are admitted; as if a man could be half innocent, and half guilty, that is, half punishable and half absolvable. It is in these cases that torture should exercise its cruel power on the person of the accused, the witnesses, and even his whole family, as, with unfeeling indifference, some civilians have taught, who pretend to dictate laws to nations.

Adultery is a crime which, politically considered, owes its existence to two causes, viz. pernicious laws, and the powerful attraction between the sexes. This attraction is similar in many circumstances to gravity, the spring of motion in the universe. Like this, it is diminished by distance; one regulates the motions of the body, the other of the soul. But they differ in one respect; the force of gravity decreases in proportion to the obstacles that oppose it, the other gathers strength and vigour as the obstacles increase.

If I were speaking to nations guided only by the laws of nature, I would tell them, that there is a considerable difference between adultery and all other crimes. Adultery proceeds from an abuse of that necessity which is constant and universal in human nature; a necessity anterior to the formation of society, and indeed the founder of society itself; whereas all other crimes, tend to the destruction of society, and arise from momentary passions, and not from a natural necessity. It is the opinion of those who have studied history and mankind, that this necessity is constantly in the same degree in the same climate. If this be true, useless, or rather pernicious, must all laws and customs be which tend to diminish the sum total of the effects of this passion.

Such laws would only burden one part of society, with the additional necessities of the other; but, on the contrary, wise are the laws which, following the natural course of the river, divide the stream into a number of equal branches, preventing thus both sterility and inundation.

Conjugal fidelity is always greater in proportion as marriages are more numerous and less difficult. But, when the interest or pride of families, or paternal authority, not the inclination of the parties, unite the sexes, gallantry soon breaks the slender ties, in spite of common moralists, who exclaim against the effect, whilst they pardon the cause. But these reflections are useless to those who, living in the true religion, act from sublimer motives, which correct the eternal laws of nature.

The act of adultery is a crime so instantaneous, so mysterious, and so concealed by the veil which the laws themselves have woven, a veil necessary indeed, but so transparent as to heighten rather than conceal the charms of the object, the opportunities are so frequent, and the danger of discovery so easily avoided, that it were much easier for the laws to prevent this crime, than to punish it when committed.

To every crime which, from its nature, must frequently remain unpunished, the punishment is an incentive. Such is the nature of the human mind, that difficulties, if not unsurmountable, nor too great for our natural indolence, embellish the object, and spur us on to the pursuit. They are so many barriers that confine the imagination to the object, and oblige us to consider it in every point of view. In this agitation, the mind naturally inclines and fixes itself to the most agreeable part, studiously avoiding every idea that might create disgust.

The crime of sodomy, so severely punished by the laws, and for the proof of which are employed tortures, which often triumph over innocence itself, has its source much less in the passions of man in a free and independent state than in society and a slave. It is much less the effect of a satiety in pleasures, than of that education which in order to make men useful to others, begins by making them useless to themselves. In those public seminaries, where ardent youth are carefully excluded from all commerce with the other sex, as the vigour of nature blooms, it is consumed in a manner not only useless to mankind, but which accelerates the approach of old age.

The murder of bastard children is, in like manner, the effect of a cruel dilemma, in which a woman finds herself, who has been seduced through weakness, or overcome by force. The alternative is, either her own infamy, or the death of a being who is incapable of feeling the loss of life. How can she avoid preferring the last to the inevitable misery of herself and her unhappy infant! The best method of preventing this crime would be effectually to protect the weak woman from that tyranny which exaggerates all vices that cannot be concealed under the cloak of virtue.

I do not pretend to lessen that just abhorrence which these crimes deserve, but to discover the sources from whence they spring; and I think I may draw the following conclusion: That the punishment of a crime cannot be just, that is necessary, if the laws have not endeavoured to prevent that crime by the best means which times and circumstances would allow.

Of Suicide

***

Suicide is a crime which seems not to admit of punishment, properly speaking; for it cannot be inflicted but on the innocent, or upon an insensible dead body. In the first case, it is unjust and tyrannical, for political liberty supposes all punishments entirely personal; in the second, it has the same effect, by way of example, as the scourging a statue. Mankind love life too well; the objects that surround them, the seducing phantom of pleasure, and hope, that sweetest error of mortals, which makes men swallow such large draughts of evil, mingled with a very few drops of good, allure them too strongly, to apprehend that this crime will ever be common from its unavoidable impunity. The laws are obeyed through fear of punishment, but death destroys all sensibility. What motive then can restrain the desperate hand of suicide?

He who kills himself does a less injury to society than he who quits his country for ever; for the other leaves his property behind him, but this carries with him at least a part of his substance. Besides, as the strength of society consists in the number of citizens, he who quits one nation to reside in another, becomes a double loss. This then is the question: whether it be advantageous to society that its members should enjoy the unlimited privilege of migration?

Every law that is not armed with force, or which, from circumstances, must be ineffectual, should not be promulgated. Opinion, which reigns over the minds of men, obeys the slow and indirect impressions of the legislator, but resists them when violently and directly applied; and useless laws communicate their insignificance to the most salutary, which are regarded more as obstacles to be surmounted than as safeguards of the public good. But further, our perceptions being limited, by enforcing the observance of laws which are evidently useless, we destroy the influence of the most salutary.

From this principle a wise dispenser of public happiness may draw some useful consequences, the explanation of which would carry me too far from my subject, which is to prove the inutility of making the nation a prison. Such a law is vain; because, unless inaccessible rocks or impassible seas divide the country from all others, how will it be possible to secure every point of the circumference, or how will you guard the guards themselves? Besides, this crime once committed cannot be punished; and to punish it before hand would be to punish the intention and not the action, the will, which is entirely out of the power of human laws. To punish the absent by confiscating his effects, besides the facility of collusion, which would inevitably be the case, and which, without tyranny, could not be prevented, would put a stop to all commerce with other nations. To punish the criminal when he returns, would be to prevent him from repairing the evil he had already done to society, by making his absence perpetual. Besides, any prohibition would increase the desire of removing, and would infallibly prevent strangers from settling in the country.

What must we think of a government which has no means but fear to keep its subjects in their own country, to which, by the first impressions of their infancy, they are so strongly attached. The most certain method of keeping men at home is to make them happy; and it is the interest of every state to turn the balance, not only of commerce, but of felicity, in favour of its subjects. The pleasures of luxury are not the principle sources of this happiness, though, by preventing the too great accumulation of wealth in a few hands, they become a necessary remedy against the too great inequality of individuals, which always increases with the progress of society.

When the populousness of a country does not increase in proportion to its extent, luxury favours despotism for where men are most dispersed there is least industry, and where there is least industry the dependence of the poor upon the luxury of the rich is greatest, and the union of the oppressed against the oppressors is least to be feared. In such circumstances, rich and powerful men more easily command distinction, respect, and service, by which they are raised to a greater height above the poor; for men are more independent the less they are observed, and are least observed when most numerous. On the contrary, when the number of people is too great in proportion to the extent of a country, luxury is a check to despotism; because it is a spur to industry, and because the labour of the poor affords so many pleasures to the rich, that they disregard the luxury of ostentation, which would remind the people of their dependence. Hence we see, that, in vast and depopulated states, the luxury of ostentation prevails over that of convenience; but in countries more populous, the luxury of convenience tends constantly to diminish the luxury of ostentation.

The pleasures of luxury have this inconvenience, that though they employ a great number of hands, yet they are only enjoyed by a few, whilst the rest who do not partake of them, feel the want more sensibly on comparing their state with that of others. Security and liberty, restrained by the laws, are the basis of happiness, and when attended by these, the pleasures of luxury favour population, without which they become the instruments of tyranny. As the most noble and generous animals fly to solitude and inaccessible deserts, and abandon the fertile plains to man their greatest enemy, so men reject pleasure itself when offered by the hand of tyranny.

But, to return:– If it be demonstrated that the laws which imprison men in their own country are vain and unjust, it will be equally true of those which punish suicide; for that can only be punished after death, which is in the power of God alone; but it is no crime with regard to man, because the punishment falls on an innocent family. If it be objected, that the consideration of such a punishment may prevent the crime, I answer, that he who can calmly renounce the pleasure of existence, who is so weary of life as to brave the idea of eternal misery, will never be influenced by the more distant and less powerful considerations of family and children.

Of Smuggling

***

Smuggling is a real offence against the sovereign and the nation; but the punishment should not brand the offender with infamy, because this crime is not infamous in the public opinion. By inflicting infamous punishments for crimes that are not reputed so, we destroy that idea where it may be useful. If the same punishment be decreed for killing a pheasant as for killing a man, or for forgery, all difference between those crimes will shortly vanish. It is thus that moral sentiments are destroyed in the heart of man; sentiments, the work of many ages and of much bloodshed; sentiments that are so slowly and with so much difficulty produced, and for the establishment of which such sublime motives and such an apparatus of ceremonies were thought necessary. This crime is owing to the laws themselves; for the higher the duties the greater is the advantage, and consequently the temptation; which temptation is increased by the facility of perpetration, when the circumference that is guarded is of great extent, and the merchandise prohibited is small in bulk. The seizure and loss of the goods attempted to be smuggled, together with those that are found along with them, is just, but it would be better to lessen the duty, because men risk only in proportion to the advantage expected.

This crime being a theft of what belongs to the prince, and consequently to the nation, why is it not attended with infamy? I answer, that crimes which men consider as productive of no bad consequences to themselves, do not interest them sufficiently to excite their indignation. The generality of mankind, upon whom remote consequences make no impression, do not see the evil that may result from the practice of smuggling, especially if they reap from it any present advantage. They only perceive the loss sustained by the prince. They are not then interested in refusing their esteem to the smuggler, as to one who has committed a theft or a forgery, or other crimes, by which they themselves may suffer, from this evident principle, that a sensible being only interests himself in those evils with which he is acquainted.

Shall this crime then, committed by one who has nothing to lose, go unpunished? No. There are certain species of smuggling, which so particularly affect the revenue, a part of government so essential, and managed with so much difficulty, that they deserve imprisonment, or even slavery; but yet of such a nature as to be proportioned to the crime. For example, it would be highly unjust, that a smuggler of tobacco should suffer the same punishment with a robber or assassin; but it would be most conformable to the nature of the offence, that the produce of his labour should be applied to the use of the crown, which he intended to defraud.

Of Sanctuaries

***

ARE sanctuaries just? Is a convention between nations mutually to give up their criminals useful?

In the whole extent of a political state there should be no place independent of the laws. Their power should follow every subject, as the shadow follows the body. Sanctuaries and impunity differ only in degree, and as the effect of punishments depends more on their certainty than their greatness, men are more strongly invited to crimes by sanctuaries than they are deterred by punishment. To increase the number of sanctuaries is to erect so many little sovereignties; for where the laws have no power, new bodies will be formed in opposition to the public good, and a spirit established contrary to that of the state. History informs us, that from the use of sanctuaries have arisen the greatest revolutions in kingdoms and in opinions.

Some have pretended, that in whatever country a crime, that is, an action contrary to the laws of society, be committed, the criminal may be justly punished for it in any other; as if the character of subject were indelible, or synonymous with or worse than that of slave; as if a man could live in one country and be subject to the laws of another, or be accountable for his actions to two sovereigns, or two codes of laws often contradictory. There are also those who think, that an act of cruelty committed, for example, at Constantinople may be punished at Paris, for this abstracted reason, that he who offends humanity should have enemies in all mankind, and be the object of universal execration; as if judges were to be the knights-errant of human nature in general, rather than guardians of particular conventions between men. The place of punishment can certainly be no other than that where the crime was committed; for the necessity of punishing an individual for the general good, subsists there, and there only. A villain, if he has not broke through the conventions of a society, of which, by my supposition, he was not a member, may be feared, and by force banished and excluded from that society, but ought not to be formally punished by the laws, which were only intended to maintain the social compact, and not to punish the intrinsic malignity of actions.

Whether it be useful that nations should mutually deliver up their criminals? Although the certainty of there being no part of the earth where crimes are not punished, may be a means of preventing them, I shall not pretend to determine this question, until laws more conformable to the necessities, and rights of humanity, and until milder punishments, and the abolition of the arbitrary power of opinion, shall afford security to virtue and innocence when oppressed; and until tyranny shall be confined to the plains of Asia, and Europe acknowledge the universal empire of reason by which the interests of sovereigns and subjects are best united.

Of Rewards for apprehending or killing Criminals

***

Let us now inquire, whether it be advantageous to society, to set a price on the head of a criminal, and so to make of every citizen an executioner? If the offender hath taken refuge in another state, the sovereign encourages his subjects to commit a crime, and to expose themselves to a just punishment; he insults that nation, and authorises the subjects to commit on their neighbours similar usurpations. If the criminal still remain in his own country, to set a price upon his head is the strongest proof of the weakness of the government. He who has strength to defend himself will not purchase the assistance of another. Besides, such an edict confounds all the ideas of virtue and morality, already too wavering in the mind of man. At one time treachery is punished by the laws, at another encouraged. With one hand the legislator strengthens the ties of kindred and friendship, and with the other rewards the violation of both. Always in contradiction with himself, now he invites the suspecting minds of men to mutual confidence, and now he plants distrust in every heart. To prevent one crime he gives birth to a thousand. Such are the expedients of weak nations, whose laws are like temporary repairs to a tottering fabric. On the contrary, as a nation becomes more enlightened, honesty and mutual confidence become more necessary, and are daily tending to unite with sound policy. Artifice, cabal, and obscure and indirect actions are more easily discovered, and the interest of the whole is better secured against the passions of the individual.

Even the times of ignorance, when private virtue was encouraged by public morality, may afford instruction and example to more enlightened ages, But laws which reward treason excite clandestine war and mutual distrust, and oppose that necessary union of morality and policy which is the foundation of happiness and universal peace.

Of Attempts, Accomplices, and Pardon

***

The laws do not punish the intention; nevertheless, an attempt, which manifests the intention of committing a crime, deserves a punishment, though less, perhaps, than if the crime were actually perpetrated. The importance of preventing even attempts to commit a crime sufficiently authorises a punishment; but, as there may be an interval of time between the attempt and the execution, it is proper to reserve the greater punishment for the actual commission, that even after the attempt there may be a motive for desisting.

In like manner, with regard to the accomplices, they ought not to suffer so severe a punishment as the immediate perpetrator of the crime: but this for a different reason. When a number of men unite, and run a common risk, the greater the danger, the more they endeavour to distribute it equally. Now, if the principals be punished more severely than the accessories, it will prevent the danger from being equally divided, and will increase the difficulty of finding a person to execute the crime, as his danger is greater by the difference of the punishment. There can be but one exception to this rule, and that is, when the principal receives a reward from the accomplices. In that case, as the difference of the danger is compensated, the punishment should be equal. These reflections may appear too refined to those who do not consider, that it is of great importance that the laws should leave the associates as few means as possible of agreeing among themselves.

In some tribunals a pardon is offered to an accomplice in a great crime, if he discover his associates. This expedient has its advantages and disadvantages. The disadvantages are, that the law authorises treachery, which is detested even by the villains themselves, and introduces crimes of cowardice, which are much more pernicious to a nation than crimes of courage. Courage is not common, and only wants a benevolent power to direct it to the public good. Cowardice, on the contrary, is a frequent, self-interested, and contagious evil, which can never be improved into a virtue. Besides, the tribunal which has recourse to this method, betrays its fallibility, and the laws their weakness, by imploring the assistance of those by whom they are, violated.

The advantages are, that it prevents great crimes, the effects of which being public, and the perpetrators concealed, terrify the people. It also contributes to prove, that he who violates the laws, which are public conventions, will also violate private compacts. It appears to me that a general law, promising a reward to every accomplice who discovers his associates, would be better than a special declaration in every particular case; because it would prevent the union of those villains, as it would inspire a mutual distrust, and each would be afraid of exposing himself alone to danger. The accomplice, however, should be pardoned, on condition of transportation. – But it is in vain that I torment myself with endeavouring to extinguish the remorse I feel in attempting to induce the sacred laws, the monument of public confidence, the foundation of human morality, to authorise dissimulation and perfidy. But what an example does it offer to a nation to see the interpreters of the laws break their promise of pardon, and on the strength of learned subtleties, and to the scandal of public faith, drag him to punishment who hath accepted of their invitation! Such examples are not uncommon, and this is the reason that political society is regarded as a complex machine, the springs of which are moved

at pleasure by the most dexterous or most powerful.

Of a particular Kind of Crimes

***

The reader will perceive that I have omitted speaking of a certain class of crimes which has covered Europe with blood, and raised up those horrid piles, from whence, amidst clouds of whirling smoke, the groans of human victims, the crackling of their bones, and the frying of their still panting bowels, were a pleasing spectacle and agreeable harmony to the fanatic multitude. But men of understanding will perceive that the age and country in which I live, will not permit me to inquire into the nature of this crime. It were too tedious and foreign to my subject to prove the necessity of a perfect uniformity of opinions in a state, contrary to the examples of many nations; to prove that opinions, which differ from one another only in some subtle and obscure distinctions, beyond the reach of human capacity, may nevertheless disturb the public tranquillity, unless one only religion be established by authority; and that some opinions, by being contrasted and opposed to each other, in their collision strike out the truth; whilst others, feeble in themselves, require the support of power and authority. It would, I say, carry me too far, where I to prove, that, how odious soever is the empire of force over the opinions of mankind, from whom it only obtains dissimulation followed by contempt, and although it may seem contrary to the spirit of humanity and brotherly love, commanded us by reason, and authority, which we more respect, it is nevertheless necessary and indispensable. We are to believe, that all these paradoxes are solved beyond a doubt, and are conformable to the true interest of mankind, if practised by a lawful authority. I write only of crimes which violate the laws of nature and the social contract, and not of sins, even the temporal punishments of which must be determined from other principles than those of limited human philosophy.

Of false Ideas of Utility

***

A principal source of errors and injustice are false ideas of utility. For example: that legislator has false ideas of utility who considers particular more than general conveniencies, who had rather command the sentiments of mankind than excite them, and dares say to reason, 'Be thou a slave'; who would sacrifice a thousand real advantages to the fear of an imaginary or trifling inconvenience; who would deprive men of the use of fire for fear of their being burnt, and of water for fear of their being drowned; and who knows of no means of preventing evil but by destroying it.

The laws of this nature are those which forbid to wear arms, disarming those only who are not disposed to commit the crime which the laws mean to prevent. Can it be supposed, that those who have the courage to violate the most sacred laws of humanity, and the most important of the code, will respect the less considerable and arbitrary injunctions, the violation of which is so easy, and of so little comparative importance? Does not the execution of this law deprive the subject of that personal liberty, so dear to mankind and to the wise legislator? and does it not subject the innocent to all the disagreeable circumstances that should only fall on the guilty? It certainly makes the situation of the assaulted worse, and of the assailants better, and rather encourages than prevents murder, as it requires less courage to attack unarmed than armed persons.

It is a false idea of utility that would give to a multitude of sensible beings that symmetry and order which inanimate matter is alone capable of receiving; to neglect the present, which are the only motives that act with force and constancy on the multitude for the more distant, whose impressions are weak and transitory, unless increased by that strength of imagination so very uncommon among mankind. Finally, that is a false idea of utility which, sacrificing things to names, separates the public good from that of individuals.

There is this difference between a state of society and a state of nature, that a savage does no more mischief to another than is necessary to procure some benefit to himself: but a man in society is sometimes tempted, from a fault in the laws, to injure another without any prospect of advantage. The tyrant inspires his vassals with fear and servility, which rebound upon him with double force, and are the cause of his torment. Fear, the more private and domestic it is, the less dangerous is it to him who makes it the instrument of his happiness; but the more it is public, and the greater number of people it affects, the greater is the probability that some mad, desperate, or designing person will seduce others to his party by flattering expectations; and this will be the more easily accomplished as the danger of the enterprise will be divided amongst a greater number, because the value the unhappy set upon their existence is less, as their misery is greater.

Of the Sciences

***

Would you prevent crimes? Let liberty be attended with knowledge. As knowledge extends, the disadvantages which attend it diminish and the advantages increase. A daring impostor, who is always a man of some genius, is adored by the ignorant populace, and despised by men of understanding. Knowledge facilitates the comparison of objects, by showing them in different points of view. When the clouds of ignorance are dispelled by the radiance of knowledge, authority trembles, but the force of the laws remains immovable. Men of enlightened understanding must necessarily approve those useful conventions which are the foundation of public safety; they compare with the highest satisfaction, the inconsiderable portion of liberty of which they are deprived with the sum total sacrificed by others for their security; observing that they have only given up the pernicious liberty of injuring their fellow-creatures, they bless the throne, and the laws upon which it is established.

It is false that the sciences have always been prejudicial to mankind. When they were so, the evil was inevitable. The multiplication of the human species on the face of the earth introduced war, the rudiments of arts, and the first laws, which were temporary compacts, arising from necessity, and perishing with it. This was the first philosophy, and its few elements were just, as indolence and want of sagacity in the early inhabitants of the world preserved them from error.

But necessities increasing with the number of mankind, stronger and more lasting impressions were necessary to prevent their frequent relapses into a state of barbarity, which became every day more fatal. The first religious errors, which peopled the earth with false divinities, and created a world of invisible beings to govern the visible creation, were of the utmost service to mankind. The greatest benefactors to humanity were those who dared to deceive, and lead pliant ignorance to the foot of the altar. By presenting to the minds of the vulgar things out of the reach of their senses, which fled as they pursued, and always eluded their grasp which as, they never comprehended, they never despised, their different passions were united, and attached to a single object. This was the first transition of all nations from their savage state. Such was the necessary, and perhaps the only bond of all societies at their first formation. I speak not of the chosen people of God, to whom the most extraordinary miracles and the most signal favours supplied the place of human policy. But as it is the nature of error to subdivide itself ad infinitum, so the pretended knowledge which sprung from it, transformed mankind into a blind fanatic multitude, jarring and destroying each other in the labyrinth in which they were inclosed: hence it is not wonderful that some sensible and philosophic minds should regret the ancient state of barbarity. This was the first epoch, in which knowledge, or rather opinions, were fatal.

The second may be found in the difficult and terrible passage from error to truth, from darkness to light. The violent shock between a mass of errors useful to the few and powerful, and the truths so important to the many and the weak, with the fermentation of passions excited on that occasion, were productive of infinite evils to unhappy mortals. In the study of history, whose principal periods, after certain intervals, much resemble each other, we frequently find, in the necessary passage from the obscurity of ignorance to the light of philosophy, and from tyranny to liberty, its natural consequence, one generation sacrificed to the happiness of the next. But when this flame is extinguished, and the world delivered from its evils, truth, after a very slow progress, sits down with monarchs on the throne, and is worshipped in the assemblies of nations. Shall we then believe, that light diffused among the people is more destructive than darkness, and that the knowledge of the relation of things can ever be fatal to mankind?

Ignorance may indeed be less fatal than a small degree of knowledge, because this adds to the evils of ignorance, the inevitable errors of a confined view of things on this side the bounds of truth; but a man of enlightened understanding, appointed guardian of the laws, is the greatest blessing that a sovereign can bestow on a nation. Such a man is accustomed to behold truth, and not to fear it; unacquainted with the greatest part of those imaginary and insatiable necessities which so often put virtue to the proof, and accustomed to contemplate mankind from the most elevated point of view, he considers the nation as his family, and his fellow-citizens as brothers; the distance between the great and the vulgar appears to him the less as the number of mankind he has in view is greater.

The philosopher has necessities and interests unknown to the vulgar, and the chief of these is not to belie in public the principles he taught in obscurity, and the habit of loving virtue for its own sake. A few such philosophers would constitute the happiness of a nation; which however would be but of short duration, unless by good laws the number were so increased as to lessen the probability of an improper choice.

Of Magistrates

***

Another method of preventing crimes is, to make the observance of the laws, and not their violation, the interest of the magistrate.

The greater the number of those who constitute the tribunal, the less is the danger of corruption; because the attempt will be more difficult, and the power and temptation of each individual will be proportionably less. If the sovereign, by pomp and the austerity of edicts, and by refusing to hear the complaints of the oppressed, accustom his subjects to respect the magistrates more than the laws, the magistrates will gain indeed, but it will be at the expense of public and private security.

Of rewards

***

Yet another method of preventing crimes is, to reward virtue. Upon this subject the laws of all nations are silent. If the rewards proposed by academies for the discovery of useful truths have increased our knowledge, and multiplied good books, is it not probable that rewards, distributed by the beneficent hand of a sovereign, would also multiply virtuous actions. The coin of honour is inexhaustible, and is abundantly fruitful in the hands of a prince who distributes it wisely.

Of Education

***

Finally, the most certain method of preventing crimes is, to perfect the system of education. But this is an object too vast, and exceeds my plan; an object, if I may venture to declare it, which is so intimately connected with the nature of government, that it will always remain a barren spot, cultivated only by a few wise men.

A great man, who is persecuted by that world he hath enlightened, and to whom we are indebted for many important truths, hath most amply detailed the principal maxims of useful education. This chiefly consists in presenting to the mind a small number of select objects, in substituting the originals for the copies both of physical and moral phenomena, in leading the pupil to virtue by the easy road of sentiment, and in withholding him from evil by the infallible power of necessary inconveniences, rather than by command, which only obtains a counterfeit and momentary obedience.

Of Pardons

***

As punishments become more mild, clemency and pardon are less necessary. Happy the nation in which they will be considered as dangerous. Clemency, which has often been deemed a sufficient substitute for every other virtue in sovereigns, should be excluded in a perfect legislation, where punishments are mild, and the proceedings in criminal cases regular and expeditious. This truth will seem cruel to those who live in countries where, from the absurdity of the laws and the severity of punishments, pardons and the clemency of the prince are necessary. It is indeed one of the noblest prerogatives of the throne, but, at the same time, a tacit disapprobation of the laws. Clemency is a virtue which belongs to the legislator, and not to the executor of the laws; a virtue which ought to shine in the code, and not in private judgment. To shew mankind that crimes are sometimes pardoned, and that punishment is not the necessary consequence, is to nourish the flattering hope of impunity, and is the cause of their considering every punishment inflicted as an act of injustice and oppression. The prince in pardoning gives up the public security in favour of an individual, and, by his ill-judged benevolence, proclaims a public act of impunity. Let, then, the executors of the laws be inexorable, but let the legislator be tender, indulgent, and humane. He is a wise architect who erects his edifice on the foundation of self-love, and contrives that the interest of the public shall be the interest of each individual, who is not obliged, by particular laws and irregular proceedings, to separate the public good from that of individuals, and erect the image of public felicity on the basis of fear and distrust; but, like a wise philosopher, he will permit his brethren to enjoy in quiet that small portion of happiness, which the immense system, established by the first cause, permits them to taste on this earth, which is but a point in the universe.

A small crime is sometimes pardoned if the person offended chooses to forgive the offender. This may be an act of good nature and humanity, but it is contrary to the good of the public: for although a private citizen may dispense with satisfaction for the injury he has received, he cannot remove the necessity of example. The right of punishing belongs not to any individual in particular, but to society in general, or the sovereign. He may re-

nounce his own portion of this right, but cannot give up that of others.

Conclusion

I conclude with this reflection, that the severity of punishments ought to be in proportion to the state of the nation. Among a people hardly yet emerged from barbarity, they should be most severe, as strong impressions are required; but, in proportion as the minds of men become softened by their intercourse in society, the severity of punishments should be diminished, if it be intended that the necessary relation between the object and the sensation should be maintained.

From what I have written results the following general theorem, of considerable utility, though not conformable to custom, the common legislator of nations:

That a punishment may not be an act of violence, of one, or of many, against a private member of society, it should be public, immediate, and necessary, the least possible in the case given, proportioned to the crime, and determined by the laws.

www.ReadHowYouWant.com

You can buy our **Large Type** and **EasyRead** books from our www.ReadHowYouWant.com website, from websites like Amazon.com and through your UK and North American bookshop.

EasyRead books are designed to make your reading easy and enjoyable. **EasyRead** books are published in different font sizes, so you can select the font size best for you.

EasyRead is for people with normal eyesight who want books in an easy-to-read format.

EasyRead Comfort is for people who find reading small print tiring but do not need large print.

EasyRead Large is for people who find it easier to read larger print.

EasyRead Large Bold is for people with retinal problems who need to read high contrast text.

EasyRead Super Large is for people who require large and dense format, available in 18pt, 20pt and 24pt.

The **EasyRead** font, character, word and line spacing have all been set to make it as easy as possible both to recognize a word, and to run your eye along a line of text without losing your place. We split as few words as possible at line ends, as split words make reading harder and can be annoying. For out-of-copyright books, words have been changed to modern spelling (where the sense is not affected), and the original hyphenation of compound words has been retained where this improves word recognition or sense.

With most things you buy, you get a choice, and you can choose the make and model that suits best. There is a big exception – books. You don't get to choose a format that is easy for you to read – you have to read the format the publisher selects.

This **"One Size Fits All"** paradigm **no longer** need apply to books.

At www.ReadHowYouWant.com, you can order a book just as you want it, so you can read it easily. You can choose nearly any format, and at a surprisingly low cost, because of a technical breakthrough that allows us to typeset an individual book automatically, print and bind the book and have it quickly sent directly to you.

You can have your book in **Talking Book** formats **(DAISY or MP3)** or as an **E-book** or in **Braille**.

We have developed totally new visual formats which we hope will help people with **dyslexia** and other print reading disabilities. Look at www.ReadHowYo uWant.com for more information.

Made in United States
Troutdale, OR
11/03/2026

56844441R00095